How to Deal With an Angry Teenager

They Are Not Just Being Assholes:

Tips on Parenting an Angry Teenager and Understanding Why Your Teenager Is Angry

Rebecca Flag - Dawn Publishing House

© Copyright 2022 - All rights reserved.

The content contained within this book may not be reproduced, duplicated or transmitted without direct written permission from the author or the publisher.

Under no circumstances will any blame or legal responsibility be held against the publisher, or author, for any damages, reparation, or monetary loss due to the information contained within this book, either directly or indirectly.

Legal Notice:

This book is copyright protected. It is only for personal use. You cannot amend, distribute, sell, use, quote or paraphrase any part, or the content within this book, without the consent of the author or publisher.

Disclaimer Notice:

Please note the information contained within this document is for educational and entertainment purposes only. All effort has been executed to present accurate, up to date, reliable, complete information. No warranties of any kind are declared or implied. Readers acknowledge that the author is not engaged in the rendering of legal, financial, medical or professional advice. The content within this book has been derived from various sources. Please consult a licensed professional before attempting any techniques outlined in this book.

By reading this document, the reader agrees that under no circumstances is the author responsible for any losses, direct or indirect, that are incurred as a result of the use of the information contained within this document, including, but not limited to, errors, omissions, or inaccuracies.

Table of Contents

INTRODUCTION 1

CHAPTER 1: LIFE AS A TEENAGER 5

AN IN-DEPTH LOOK INTO TEENAGE HOOD 5
    The Teenage Brain 6
    The Physical Changes a Teenager Experiences During Puberty 8
    The Social and Emotional Changes a Teenager Experiences During Puberty 12
    In Closing 17

CHAPTER 2: WHY IS MY TEENAGER SO ANGRY ALL THE TIME? 19

UNDERSTANDING YOUR REBELLIOUS TEEN 19
    Reason 1: Low Self-Esteem 20
    Reason 2: Family Conflict 26
    Reason 3: Death of a Loved One 27
    Reason 4: Drugs and Alcohol Use 29
    Reason 5: Mental Health Issues, Behavioral Disorders and Eating Disorders 31

CHAPTER 3: WARNING! YOUR TEENAGER IS IN TROUBLE 41

SIGNS THAT INDICATE YOUR TEENAGER IS HEADED DOWN THE WRONG ROAD 41
    Sign 1: Drastic Changes in Their Academic Performance 42
    Sign 2: Isolating Themselves and Losing Interest In Their Hobbies 43
    Sign 3: Being Disrespectful and Hurtful Towards Others 44
    Sign 4: Lack of Drive and Ambition to Pursue Their Dreams 44
    Sign 5: Bullying Other Kids 45
    Sign 6: Neglecting Their Personal Hygiene 46
    Sign 7: Self-Injury 47
    Sign 8: Emotional Outbursts 47
    Sign 9: Stealing 48
    Sign 10: Promiscuous Behavior 49

CHAPTER 4: WHEN TECHNOLOGY HELPS YOUR TEEN BECOME REBELLIOUS 51

TECHNOLOGY AND TEENAGERS 51
WHY ARE TEENAGERS SO ADDICTED TO TECHNOLOGY? 52
    Why Do Teenagers Use Technology? 52
    How Does Technology Impact the Human Brain? 53
    How Does Technology Impact the Physical Health of Your Teenager? 55
SOCIAL MEDIA AND ITS CONNECTION TO TEENAGE REBELLION 56

How are Teenagers Influenced by Social Media? 57
The Pros and Cons of Teenage Social Media Use 58

CHAPTER 5: HOW YOU CAN HELP YOUR TEENAGER THROUGH THIS PHASE..... 63

TIPS TO HELP YOU BECOME MORE SUPPORTIVE AND UNDERSTANDING TOWARDS YOUR
TEENAGER 63
What Your Responsibilities Are as a Parent 64
What You Should Avoid Doing as a Parent 71
Teenagers and COVID-19 75

CHAPTER 6: REBUILDING YOUR RELATIONSHIP WITH YOUR TEENAGER 83

HEALING WOUNDS AND OPENING HEARTS 83
The Wrong Parenting Styles 84
How to Repair a Broken Relationship With Your Teenager 90
Practical Exercises to Help You Become a Better Parent 94

CONCLUSION 97

REFERENCES 99

IMAGE REFERENCES 100

Introduction

Troubled teenagers are every parent's worst nightmare. They are in a league of their own, often misunderstood and not taken seriously. Similar was the situation between Kat and her mother, who were constantly fighting and at each other's throats almost every day. Kat was a 16-year-old who lived with her mom and younger sister. Kat's father passed away when she was around 11 years old, and her mom had to work two jobs just to make ends meet for the family. While her mom was away at work, Kat had to practically raise her sister all by herself. She missed out on a lot of her childhood because she had to step up and become responsible for her sister and for their home. She had many questions about life, she was growing into a young woman, and she needed guidance from her mom about things that were happening to her body.

Since her mom wasn't around, Kat had to figure things out for herself, and most of the time she would confide in her neighbor Beth, who was 19. Beth helped Kat in whatever way she could, and the two became fairly close over the years. When Kat turned 15, she and her mom could not see eye to eye any longer. They would argue daily about everything, and this affected Kat's ability to study well and focus on school. Somehow, Kat had anger inside her towards her mother that she never really knew was there. Whenever they disagreed about something, Kat would become consumed by it. She eventually started pushing her mom away, blaming her for not being there when she needed her. This led to a complete breakdown in communication between parent and child, which then led to more misunderstandings.

Kat's mom couldn't understand where this anger was coming from. She assumed that Kat was just acting out because she didn't get her way. So instead of having a conversation with her daughter about their issues, she chose to ignore them as long as Kat was willing to give in and behave. This approach heightened the hostility between mother and daughter. Kat felt even more alone and unloved by her mom, so she decided to seek acceptance and comfort with the wrong kind of friends; Beth being one of them. Kat became involved in alcohol use and experimented with drugs. Whenever she was with Beth, she felt loved and accepted. The high she experienced from drugs and alcohol helped her forget all about her problems. From here on, everything only got worse. A troubled teenager, a stressed out mom, both could not understand each other, and neither were willing to talk about their issues.

There are so many families around the world who are experiencing similar issues as Kat and her mom. Teenagers are a unique brand of human beings. From the way they talk to the ways they think and act, everything is different, and this is why they are misunderstood by the people around them. If you're reading this book, it's probably because you have a troubled teenager on your hands, and you are looking for a way to help them. Well, you have made a good decision by choosing this book to help you deal with your angry teenager. Inside, you will learn about the inner workings of a teenager's mind. You will understand what a teenager goes through, and what makes them so angry all the time. We have also provided you with ways that can help you be patient with your teenager, even when you feel like giving them the whooping of a lifetime. So get ready—you are going to learn a lot about your teenager from this moment on!

Chapter 1:
Life as a Teenager

An In-Depth Look into Teenage hood

A teenager's life seems to always be changing. From their constant mood swings and irritability to their attitude and interests in certain activities. It can be hard for parents to understand what is going on in their teenager's mind, for the most part; the age gap between parent and child makes it difficult for them to connect on a deeper level. However, parents must realize that they were teenagers once, too. They know what it's like to experience teenage hood because they have already gone through that phase in their lives. Fairly speaking, a parent's experience would be poles apart from their teenager's experience because of the era in which they grew up, but the emotions and physical changes would be very similar. In this chapter, you will learn about what changes a teenager goes through, both physically and emotionally, and you will get a better idea of how these changes impact their lives.

The Teenage Brain

A few years ago, Theresa's 16-year-old son got into an accident and wrote off his car. A few years later, her 14-year-old daughter decided to dye her hair a dark blue and hot pink color. Theresa just couldn't understand what her kids were thinking. Little did she realize, their impulsive behavior was attributed to the changes in a teenage brain. A neurologist from the University of Pennsylvania, Francis E. Jensen, decided to perform an in-depth study of the teenage brain. She wanted to understand how teenage brains worked and processed thoughts. Francis believed that parents could better understand their teenagers just by knowing what goes on in their heads. (Forster, 2017)

Sometimes, parents expect too much from their teenagers, without being aware of how developed their brains are. There are many factors that play a part in brain development, such as age, health and wellbeing, nourishment, the environment they are growing up in, and what they're exposed to daily. Parents have to remember that their teenagers are not adults yet. Teenage hood is the phase in which people transition from childhood to adulthood. This is a crucial time in their lives. They are growing physically, are becoming more mature emotionally, and are discovering themselves for the first time ever. This is a tremendous amount of work for the human brain, as you can imagine.

A Work in Progress

From the moment you were born, your brain has been growing and developing steadily. So much so, that by the time you've reached six years old, most of your brain has been fully developed—95% to be precise—except for the gray part of your brain which is the area responsible for thinking, planning, organizing, and judgment. This part of the brain continues to thicken and develop throughout your childhood. When girls reach age 11 and boys reach age 12, the adolescence phase, the gray matter, also known as the frontal lobe, reaches its highest point in growth; after this it starts to thin and prune out. During adolescence, teenagers have so much potential to learn and develop new skills. This is the time in their lives when they can make use of all the extra cells and connections that have been made available by the development of the gray matter.

If teenagers don't use up these cells, they will wither and die away once adolescence has passed. For instance, if a teenager has been involved in playing chess, or learning about a musical instrument, or studying daily, then these are the connections that will stay with them in the long term. However, if they were spending their time watching TV or playing video games, then those connections will remain with them as well, long term. That's why it is so important that teenagers engage in meaningful activities during the adolescent phase, because it determines what their abilities and skills will be later on in life. From the beginning of puberty, until the time a teenager enters adulthood, is a crucial phase where the brain develops exceptionally. A teenager can be extremely vulnerable during this time, because whatever they are exposed to will determine who they become as a person.

During the teen years, the frontal lobe of the brain has not been fully developed just yet. It's still a work in progress, which means teenagers are not capable of making the right decisions regarding their behavior and their lives. Parents should not expect them to think like an adult or act like one, because they cannot comprehend situations the way that adults do. Their brains are still in the process of being built—you wouldn't remove a cake early out of the oven and expect it to be fully cooked, after all. There is a time and process for all things to grow into their full potential, and a teenager is no exception. How a teenager chooses to spend their time during this phase will greatly impact their lives. A lot of teenagers begin to experiment with drugs and alcohol during puberty, and they also become increasingly curious about sex. If they are not properly educated by their parents and teachers about sex, drugs, and alcohol, then they will not be aware of how to be safe while experimenting with these things.

Even adults are still learning and maturing as they age each year; no one can say that they know it all or that they are vastly confident about the decisions they make at any stage in their lives. As you grow older, you look back on life and feel regretful over a few stupid decisions you have made. You somehow feel like you were naive and immature when you were younger, and that contributed to the poor choices you made. In the same way, your teenager is at a place in their lives where they have no experience or wisdom to make decisions that seem right to you. They think and act according to their level of perception, and you cannot expect more of that. Your experiences and your age have played a part in helping you make better decisions, so you cannot expect your teenager to see things the way you do.

The Physical Changes a Teenager Experiences During Puberty

During puberty, teenagers experience several changes to their physical body. Many of these changes are difficult to adapt to, especially for those teenagers who have self-esteem issues. Growth spurts become a regular part of a teenager's life, and each time they look in the mirror, they will notice something new about themselves. We all have gone through this stage in our lives, and whether you are a man or woman, puberty must not have been an easy time for you. Between ages 13 and 18, a teenager will grow significantly; it's a normal part of adolescence. However, there's one thing to remember: not every teenager will grow at the same pace. Everyone is unique, so their bodies will grow differently from others. Most teenagers become insecure about their outer appearance because they look different from their friends. Let's take a look at how a teenager's body changes and develops from the age of 13 up until 18.

What Changes Will Occur During Puberty?

Puberty comes unexpectedly, and most kids don't know how to respond to it. A teenager's body will go through a transformation during this time, and it can sometimes be an embarrassing time in their lives. Boys and girls both experience puberty; however, the changes they go through are very dissimilar. Below, we highlight the main changes that boys and girls experience during adolescence.

In Boys

It can be hard to tell when a boy is going through puberty, mainly because he will experience changes that occur gradually over time.

There is no single event that can show when a male has reached puberty, as there is for girls. Puberty usually starts at around nine years old and can last all the way until age 14 without showing any signs (although this might not be the case for every boy). Some boys will display signs that they have reached puberty. One of the first changes a boy will notice is the enlargement of the testicles. The penis starts to grow a year after the testicles have enlarged. When they have reached the age of 13 or 14, they will start to notice hair growth in the pubic region. "Wet dreams," or nocturnal emissions, another significant occurrence, happen at the age of 14 and older.

At around age 15, their voices deepen and become more hoarse. Your teenager will start to sound less like a child and more like a young adult. Facial hair will start to appear on the chin and under the nose. It won't be too thick or full, but it will be noticeable. Acne might also set in during this time, appearing on the cheeks and forehead. A lot of teenagers have trouble accepting their acne, and this leads to further depletion of their self-confidence. Some teenagers make it through adolescence without experiencing acne—it's got a lot to do with hormonal changes and skin type. Acne can be severe in boys, and it usually gets worse as hormones fluctuate. The outer appearance of males also changes during puberty. They become much taller, and their shoulders become broader. If they were chubby as a kid, most of that "baby fat" will start to melt away. By the time they reach 18, they look more like an adult than a kid. Their sexual organs will have fully developed by now, and their overall facial features and structure will be more defined to look like a young man.

In Girls

Girls also experience puberty, however, the changes that occur in girls are unique and different from those experienced by boys. Each girl is different, so they might go through these changes at different times during puberty. Most girls start by the age of 12 or 13, whilst others start as early as 8 to 10. At the onset of puberty, girls will go through a lot of hormonal changes as well as physical changes to their body. One of the first signs of puberty in girls is the development of breasts. By the time a girl reaches 10 years old, her breasts will have started to grow and change. She will need her first training bra when this happens.. Thereafter, a girl will notice hair growing in her pubic region at around 10 to 11 years old.

Whilst all of these changes are significant and important, there is one change that stands apart from the rest, and this is when a girl starts menstruating. A girl's period can start anywhere from nine years old, and oftentimes it shows up unannounced. This is a significant sign that shows when a girl is transitioning into a woman, and it is a special moment that is shared between mothers and daughters. Girls also experience mild to severe acne at age 14 or 15. Hormonal changes contribute to the severity of the acne as well. Once these hormones have settled, so too, will the acne breakouts become less common. A girl's outer appearance also changes with time. They become taller, their hips and waist become wider, and their overall appearance becomes more feminine and womanly. By the time they reach age 18, they have fully developed breasts, and their sexual organs are also fully developed.

These changes don't just happen without having any impact on a teenager. Going from being a child to an adult isn't something that happens overnight. It is a whole process that takes around five to six years to complete. A teenager will not be the same at the end of this process. Along with their physical changes, their emotions and personality have also been under development. Parents need to understand the impact that these changes have on their teenager's mind and emotions. In the next section, we learn more about what emotional changes a teenager experiences during puberty. This will help you get a deeper understanding of what it is like being a teenager.

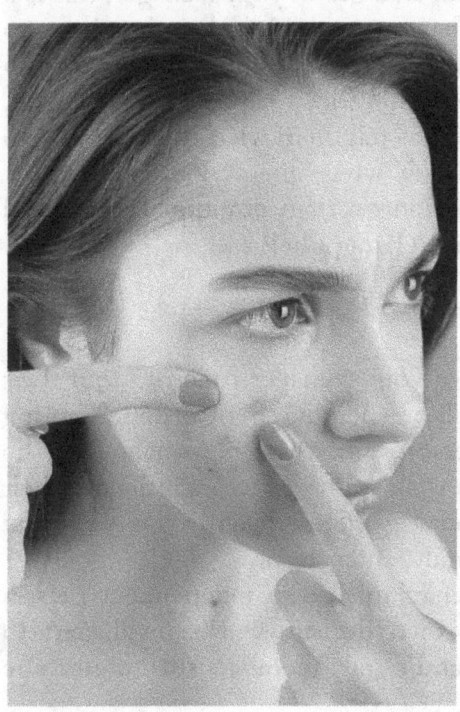

The Social and Emotional Changes a Teenager Experiences During Puberty

Adolescence is an important time in your teenager's life, and it can be emotionally draining from time to time. Your teenager is leaving behind their child-like state of mind, and growing into a more mature way of comprehending the world around them. They are newly discovering how things work, and they are learning about their bodies. This can be a lot of information to take in, and most teenagers don't understand how to process this information. During puberty, there are other areas of your teenager's life that undergo changes as well. Their social life, for example, is one of the significant areas that become affected. You, as a parent, will notice changes in your child's behavior, especially towards other family members. They will behave in a manner that is different from their usual self.

Social and Emotional Changes to Expect

When you notice emotional or social changes in your teenager, this is a good sign, because it indicates that your child is learning how to operate as an independent individual. He or she is beginning to form their own thoughts and opinions about various aspects of their lives, and they are no longer relying on you to tell them what to do or how to behave. Sometimes, parents won't know what signs to look out for that can point to their teenager experiencing certain emotional and social changes, so we have highlighted these changes below.

Social Changes:
- At this stage, you will notice your teenager trying to find their place in the world. They will be spending a lot of time figuring out who they are as a person, and their personality will be developing and changing as well. A lot of factors influence their experience, such as their gender, health, culture and background, friends and family, and school.
- Your teenager will start behaving like an independent person who wants to make their own decisions. They will start to choose the type of friends and family members they want to be

around. You will notice them becoming distant from certain friends or family members without any real reason why.
- A teenager will start to crave more responsibility, both at home and at school. They will want you to trust them to get certain things done on their own and on time. This is a common sign of social changes among adolescent teens.
- You will notice that your teenager is engaging in more risk-taking behavior. They will look for new experiences that are exciting, and during this process they will also learn about controlling their impulses.
- Your teenager will start to understand what is right from wrong, and they will develop their own set of core values and morals for themselves to follow. They will be watching your actions and behavior to help them gain a better understanding of right and wrong.
- Suddenly, you will notice that your teenager starts to ask questions frequently. They become curious about the world around them because they think that the more they know about how the world works, the easier it will be to fit in.
- Your teenager will become involved with dating, and will want to learn about their sexual identity. This doesn't necessarily mean that they are sexually active, just simply curious about love and romance.
- You will notice your teenager becoming more drawn towards social media and modern technology. Their main form of communication will be through cell phones, laptops, and other devices.

Emotional Changes:
- You will notice changes in their mood and emotions. They will become more irritable and annoyed than usual.
- Teenagers become more aware of the emotions and feelings of those around them. If you are upset over something, your teenager will be able to understand your facial expressions, tone of voice, and body language.
- Your teenager is very self-conscious about their physical appearance, which causes a lot of emotional stress and

frustration. They may complain about their bodies and expect to look exactly like their friends.
- During these emotional changes, your teenager may make decisions that could put their lives in danger, but they feel as if nothing could ever happen to them, so they don't take the consequences seriously. This is because their emotional intelligence has not been fully developed yet.
- You will notice your teenager becoming increasingly withdrawn from activities they used to love participating in, and when you try to talk to them, they will not reveal much about their feelings.
- Your teenager will choose to spend more time with their friends rather than hang out with their parents because they may feel judged or misunderstood by their parents. With their friends, they feel at ease and free to be whomever they want to be.
- Arguments will be on the rise, and conflict never seems to cease at home. Your teenager sees things from their own point of view now, and will feel even more obligated to take a stand for their beliefs.

Finding Themselves in the Midst of Chaos and Confusion

Let's, for a moment, put ourselves back in our teenage bodies. Close your eyes and picture your younger self. Young and carefree, starting on your journey into adulthood and learning about life for the first time. Feel the emotions you felt back then. Try to embrace the same mindset you used to have as a teenager. Remember all the changes you experienced, both emotionally and physically? Can you remember what your relationship was like with your parents? Did you feel like they understood you throughout your teenage years? What would you say was the most difficult part of being a teenager? As you start to remember what you were like as a teenager, think about how your own kids are experiencing their teenage years.

You should be able to relate to them on a deeper level after remembering that you were once a teenager. All of these changes that a teenager has to go through can be highly taxing on their emotions. They can easily become lost in a giant sea of confusion and frustration, desperately trying to hold on and stay afloat, but the tide is sweeping over them constantly. If there is anyone who can understand what a teenager is going through, it is the parent. They know what it's like being a teenager, and they should be able to help their own kids stay afloat so that they can pull through this tough phase. Living life as a teenager can be extremely chaotic. With all the physical and emotional changes that are taking place at the same time, it can be hard to focus. Your teenager's main goal throughout all this is to find their true identity. They will be learning a lot about their personality during their adolescent years. Going through the motions will help your teen figure out what they can handle and what they cannot. Your teen will learn about their likes and dislikes, and the only way they can do this is by exploring different aspects of life.

An important thing to remember is that the type of personality your teen creates for themselves will remain with them for the rest of their lives. They will adapt to whatever they are exposed to during this stage in their lives. If you think about it carefully, a teenager does have a lot to deal with. Peer pressure from their friends, a tremendous amount of schoolwork, trying to cope with their emotions and feelings, and dealing with their family life, all whilst trying to figure out who they really are. For a brain that is still being developed, this can cause a huge amount of strain on their mental health. It wouldn't take much for them to crack under all of this pressure, because they are only just experiencing it for the first time. It is a long, hard journey to finding their true identity and purpose in life, so it's vital that parents be patient and understanding with their teenagers during this time.

The Hard Part

Every teenager is different—this is something we all can agree on. The "hard part" of teenage hood differs from teen to teen. Some might agree that the hardest part of being a teenager is leaving behind their childhood and having to grow up, even though they aren't ready to do so. Others may say that the hardest part of being a teen is going through the physical changes. Whichever it is, the impact it has on the teenage brain will determine how well they cope with change and transformation in the future. All these hurdles that a teen goes through helps prepare them for what's to come later on in life. It makes them stronger and more resilient as individuals, and it also adds character to their personality.

A teenager is constantly focused on the present. They rarely ever think about their future, and they always think that they have plenty of time to grow up, so why not enjoy life now. This is where the impulsive behavior comes into play. The moment an idea pops into their head, they remain steadfast to make sure that they act upon that idea. This type of behavior is childish and immature, which is quite normal for a teenager. Children don't think about the consequences of their actions; they do whatever they want to d0. They don't take responsibility for their actions, and they are often unaware of how their behavior affects those around them. Leaving behind that childish nature can be very difficult for most teenagers. They have a hard time moving away from their childish ways because they feel adult life will be boring. However, change is inevitable; one way or another they are going to have to grow up and become more responsible over their lives.

Can you remember how you felt when you realized that you had to grow up and start being a responsible individual? I'm sure that you would have felt brokenhearted over the fact that your childhood days were now behind you. As a teenager, you would have experienced so many emotions that it would have been hard for you to understand what you were feeling and why you were feeling that way. Your teenager is in the same boat that you were in. They are going through the same changes you did, and they are having a hard time accepting these changes. Their emotional state will be rather fragile, and they can snap at the smallest of things. You can never tell what is going on in their heads. A teen's mind can be as complex as a maze, and no matter how you look at it, it just doesn't make sense.

In Closing

Now that you have gained a bit of insight into how a teenager develops through the years, this information should shed some light onto why teenagers behave the way they do. Their state of mind is influenced by a number of different aspects, not to mention all the changes that their bodies are experiencing. As much as you can, try to compare your experience as a teenager with that of your child's. It will help you see things from their perspective without being judgmental. In the next chapter, we focus on understanding why your teenager is so angry all the time. We explore the possible reasons behind their anger and annoyance, so you can figure out ways to help your teenager overcome their emotions.

Chapter 2:
Why Is My Teenager So Angry All the Time?

Understanding Your Rebellious Teen

When you think of the word "teenager," you may picture a 14-year-old with an angry face, dressed however they please, sitting on their mobile phone. Don't get me wrong, I'm not being biased towards teenagers; if you have a teenager walking around your house, you understand why I described them in that way. Ask any parent of a teen to describe the way their teenager behaves, and they will tell you that they are raising angry birds 24/7. An angry teenager can be compared to a time bomb that is waiting to explode. You never know what to say or how to act around them, because it's the smallest of things that get them to blow their top off. Unfortunately for these parents, life can be a complete nightmare once their children enter teenage hood.

There are many potential reasons that contribute to your teenager's anger problems. Sometimes parents overlook these issues because they don't believe that they can contribute to any of the emotional instabilities that a teenager is experiencing. However, these issues can be alleviated, if only parents paid attention to them. We fail to comprehend that each teenager is different: their maturity levels, the manner in which they react to certain situations, and their ability to regulate their emotions differ from one another. As a parent, if you truly want to figure out why your teenager is so angry all the time, you have to be willing to put aside your own anger and switch off that critical attitude. You must be willing to seek to understand, and not to judge.

Reason 1: Low Self-Esteem

Having a lack of self-confidence is fairly common among teenagers, especially in the early teen years. A teenager who has poor self-esteem cannot see anything good in themselves, even when it's clearly evident to everyone else. You can tell them how great they look in that new pair of jeans, and they would think that they look fat. These are common reactions you can expect from a teenager; every parent is aware of this. There are many transitions that a teenager goes through. One in particular is starting at a high school. They want to fit in and look like the other teenagers around them, but they don't realize that everyone else is growing at their own pace. This causes them to question their appearance and feel incomplete, when in reality they are exactly the way they should be right now in their lives. There are a lot of teenagers who quickly become depressed because of their self-esteem issues, and when this happens, it can lead to other complications.

Why Is Self-Esteem Important for Teenagers?

Positive self-esteem is essential for teenagers because it enables them to take chances on things that interest them and be confident about the decisions they make. There are many key decisions to make as a teenager, such as choosing the type of friends you want to have in your life, picking a sport or hobby to get involved in, or whether you should go on that date with Tommy from the 10th grade. These are common events that take place in a teenager's life, and it would be a shame to miss out on them because of low self-esteem. When teenagers don't have confidence in themselves, they will shy away from activities that make teenage life so exciting. Going on a first date, being a part of the football squad, or becoming a member of a great group of friends; all of these things take courage, and if teenagers don't believe in themselves, then they will never have the courage to do these things.

We all have backed down from a few risks in our lives and turned down some great opportunities, all because of fear. We were too scared that things wouldn't work out because we didn't believe in ourselves. Now, as we look back on our younger days, we have so many regrets. Your teenager is feeling the same way about themselves. They probably don't feel as if they are good enough to take a chance on anything exciting. They are afraid of failure and disappointment because they lack confidence in themselves. In order for your teenager to be the best that they can be, they have to be willing to take chances and risks in their lives. When they are confident in themselves, and when they believe that they can achieve anything, it becomes easier for them to push through difficult situations.

How Does Low Self-Esteem Affect Your Teen?

Self-esteem is a significant part of our lives. Without it, we would be lost, ambitionless human beings who just merely exist without a purpose. Not a pleasant thought, is it? Now, can you imagine your teenager feeling the exact same way? How sad and depressed they must be inside, thinking that they aren't good enough to dream dreams and have goals. These negative emotions do affect them in the long run. If your teenager's low self-esteem issues are ignored and left untreated, it could have an enormous impact on their lives.

Here are some of the problems that can occur because of low self-esteem:

- Lack of motivation to do their best in every situation.
- Loss of interest in activities they used to love being a part of.
- Poor body image and hatred towards the way their body is developing.
- Mental health issues such as depression and anxiety.
- Becoming involved in drugs and alcohol to help them forget about their pain.
- Becoming sexually active at a very young age to feel accepted.
- Frequent mood swings and irritability.

These issues must be addressed early on, in the initial stages of development. Parents should be able to recognize these signs in their teenagers; it can be hard to miss. Teenagers will sometimes try their best to hide their true feelings, and in this instance, a parent will have no way of knowing what their child is going through. Whilst experimenting with drugs and alcohol might be a normal part of being a teenager, it can point to a problem if your teenager does it continuously. Regular use of these substances could indicate that your teenager cannot function without it, and this should be addressed immediately. Low self-esteem can tremendously impact your teenager's social life, personal life, school life, and their overall health and wellbeing.

Causes of Low Self-Esteem

Low self-esteem can be brought on by a number of different aspects. Those who have issues with their self-esteem can usually track the roots back to a certain event or trauma that occurred in their lives. However, some people might block out that event because of the pain it caused them, so they cannot remember when their self-esteem issues began. Honestly speaking, we all have insecurities that we hide from the world. We weren't born with these insecurities, they formed inside of us because of the experiences we had in life. Let's look at some main reasons why teenagers develop problems with their self-esteem.

Being Around People Who Don't Care About Them

If your teenager is surrounded by people who don't show interest in their lives and who avoid spending time with them, then that can cause some major issues with their self-esteem. Your teenager needs the love and support from their friends and family so that they can get through difficult situations in their lives. Without anyone there to encourage them or make them feel empowered, your teenager will lose confidence in themselves eventually.

Bad Friends

One of the most common reasons why teenagers lose confidence in themselves is by being influenced through bad friends. Peer pressure is very real, and it exists even though teenagers are more aware of it these days. Parents don't understand how their teenager can be easily influenced to do the wrong things, even after educating them about the dangers of peer pressure. Your teenager doesn't realize that they are keeping the wrong type of friends, so when these friends try to manipulate them into doing things that they don't want to do, your teenager cannot understand it and they give in to the peer pressure thinking that it is a normal part of friendship.

When your teen becomes involved in doing things that are against their own morals and values, their self-esteem drops, and they lose confidence in themselves. This makes it hard to stand up to their friends and be firm about their choices. There will also be friends who show off their wealth and good looks, with the intention of making everyone else feel inferior and jealous of them. If your teen is involved with this type of friend, their self-esteem can take a huge hit. They will never be happy with anything you give them unless they can match up to these "showing off" friends, but they don't realize what it does to their self-esteem.

Divorce Among Parents

This is another major reason why teenagers develop low self-esteem. Divorce isn't something that can be hidden from children, especially if it is a messy one. With parents arguing constantly, they have very little time for their teenagers. Their actions and words are not chosen wisely in front of their kids, and sometimes the things that are said in a heated argument get interpreted differently by the kids. By the time they become teenagers, they carry the weight of these words with them. The trauma that is caused by divorce often leaves a permanent scar upon the self-esteem of the children involved.

When a teenager watches their parents, two of the people they love most in the world, go their separate ways, it shakes the very foundation in which their lives were built upon. And when this foundation breaks and the family splits apart, it leaves a teenager in a vulnerable position emotionally. Sometimes, they might even blame themselves for their parents getting divorced; a lot of kids do, but this isn't the truth. If your teenager has experienced a parental divorce and had trouble accepting that, then this could very well be the reason behind their anger.

Sexual or Physical Abuse

Abuse has become more common among households these days, with 16% of youth between the ages of 14 and 17 being sexually abused every year. (National Center for Victims of Crime, n.d.) No abuse is worse than the other; whether it's physical abuse, sexual abuse, or both, the trauma that is experienced by these teenagers is enough to last an entire lifetime. When teenagers are exposed to abuse from a young age, it can alter their way of thinking and the way they react to stressful situations. A victim mentality takes a hold of their mind, causing them to settle for less and remain quiet whenever they are exposed to any form of abuse.

The damage caused by sexual abuse kills something inside these teenagers that is necessary for their success in life. It steals their dignity, their pride, and their self-respect, leaving them with nothing but pure hatred for their own bodies. As an adult, that can be very hard to deal with, so I'm sure you can understand how hard it must be for a teenager. In this particular situation, it takes a lot of time and patience for a teenager to regain their self-esteem. A series of counseling sessions and support from family and friends are the only way a teen can start healing.

Inadequate Performance at School and Other Activities

If your teenager is unable to achieve good grades in school, despite trying their best, it can have a negative impact on their self-confidence. Let's say that your teenager used to be at the top of their class in elementary and middle school; however, now that they are in high school, they find it hard to achieve top results. And because of this sudden change, they lose confidence in themselves, and they start to question their abilities. Teenagers don't realize that high school isn't as easy as middle school used to be, the workload gets heavier, and the syllabus takes some time to get used to.

There are other activities that come into play when a teenager enters high school. Exciting activities such as sports, soccer, drama, chess, etc. A teenager will be drawn towards activities that match their personality and interests, and they may want to instantly succeed in these activities. However, when they are faced with failure, their confidence gets shattered and their self-esteem drops. Because of their immaturity, teenagers won't understand that failure is not permanent. Instead, they become depressed and look down on themselves.

Being Bullied

Teenagers who have been bullied by other kids generally develop low self-confidence because of the daily trauma they experience. A bully always publicly humiliates their victim, because they are trying to crush their victim's spirit by embarrassing them. This humiliation has a tremendous impact on a teenager's self-esteem. In some cases, teenagers have even taken their own lives as a result of being bullied. The emotional and physical damage caused by bullying sticks with a teenager throughout their lifetime. Even the person doing the bullying is doing it because they also lack confidence in themselves, and that is why they are inflicting pain on others—because they want other people to feel the same way they do. If you think about it clearly, one is being a bully because of their low self-esteem, whilst the other is a victim because of their low self-esteem. Whichever way you choose to look at it, there's no way that you can deny how a teenager's life is influenced by low self-esteem.

Medical Illness

Having any type of medical illness as a teenager can be very hard to live with. It can prevent them from doing all the fun stuff that teenagers usually do. This is the most crucial stage in their lives, where they learn how to socialize and make friends, create an identity for themselves, and build a foundation for their future. An illness could prevent them from doing the things they set out to do. Depending on the type of medical illness your teenager may have, it could very well restrict them from having a social life. This alone is enough to cause depression and low self-esteem in your teenager. Watching your friends and family doing the things you have always wanted to do can be heartbreaking, to say the least. Not to mention the daily struggle with taking medication and/or dealing with the discomfort of the illness.

When you have a headache or an upset tummy, those few days of being sick can seem unbearable to you. For that short period of time, you are tired, and you aren't feeling all that good about yourself, either. Imagine if you had a long term-illness. How would that affect your mindset and your attitude towards life? A teenager does not have the ability to self-regulate their emotions about their illness, so it ends up impacting them negatively. One of the first things that takes a hit is their confidence in themselves.

Reason 2: Family Conflict

Conflict and strife among family members is normal. When people disagree, they voice their concerns, and oftentimes it leads to a heated argument where things become a bit out of control. Each person has their own opinions and their own way of doing things, and when opinions clash, conflict starts. When teenagers grow up in homes where there is constant conflict, it can cause a lot of trauma to their lives, especially if the conflict exists between a parent and their teenager. Let's take a look at how conflict can impact your teenager.

How Does Conflict Impact Your Teenager?

Conflict among family can affect a teenager in many ways, and it can have both short and long-term effects on their lives. The harsh words spoken, the shouting, and the violent behavior are all part of the recipe for destruction. A teenager is not yet equipped to handle conflict in a healthy way. The way they react to it will only escalate issues and make things worse, rather than better. When faced with conflict, a teenager will act out by being aggressive or rebellious. Because they cannot process and regulate their intense feelings, they choose to become defiant as a way of getting back at you, which only causes more conflict in the home. Your teenager may start displaying signs of depression, and they may isolate themselves for hours on end. They may not want to be around the family or be a part of any activities that involve everyone being together.

When parents fight among themselves, a lot of their time and attention gets directed towards the conflict. They become so consumed by the negative emotions brought on by the conflict that they completely shut their kids out and stop paying any attention to their needs. A teenager will try to fight for their parents' attention by doing the opposite of what is expected of them. Dropping their grades at school, engaging in risky behavior, joining the wrong friend groups, and changing their physical appearance in some way or another.

Reason 3: Death of a Loved One

Though death comes as a sudden shock, there is no way to avoid it. It is inevitable and it exists for us all. Learning how to cope with grief is hard enough for adults, even when they are emotionally mature enough to handle it. But when it comes to dealing with death as a teenager, the process can be long and much more difficult to endure, especially if it is the first time losing a loved one. It can be even more devastating if they have lost a parent or a sibling, someone who was a close part of their lives. Teenagers need to be able to grieve in a healthy way so that they can overcome the loss, before letting it consume them. If your teenager has recently lost someone they love dearly, then you should look out for signs that indicate long-term grief. If your teenager is displaying any of the signs, this could mean that they aren't processing their grief properly. Here are some of the signs.

Anger and Frustration

If you notice that your teenager has become increasingly angry and frustrated long after the death of a loved one, then it could indicate that they are having a hard time dealing with their emotions by themselves. Getting involved in fights at school, lashing out at family members over trivial matters, or being angry at the deceased are common signs you should keep an eye out for. You will have to intervene and help your teenager open up and work through their feelings of anger and frustration.

Loss of Appetite

If your teenager has been skipping meals or throwing up immediately after eating, then this could indicate that they have developed an eating disorder after the death of a loved one. The shock and grief can cause appetite loss for the first few days after the loss of a loved one; however, it should not persist for weeks or months on end. This means that your teenager is not coping well with their grief.

Nightmares and Trouble Sleeping

Another sign of unhealthy grief is having recurrent nightmares about an incident involving the deceased, or not being able to sleep at all throughout the night. If you have seen your teenager awake for hours on end, unable to sleep, long after the death of a loved one, it could mean that your teen has become disturbed and overcome by their grief. Sleep is a vital part of life, and when any incident interferes with that, it usually means that the issue is serious.

Bed Wetting

Bed-wetting, in the teenage years, can be concerning for parents since it does indicate that your teenager is going through some type of trauma that is affecting them deeply. If your teenager has been wetting the bed often, you should consider seeking professional help. Typically, a therapist or child psychologist will be able to help your teen deal with their grief and process their emotions. Your teenager may try to hide the fact that they have been wetting the bed because it is embarrassing for them to open up about it, so proceed with caution and love when talking to them about it.

Reason 4: Drugs and Alcohol Use

Experimenting with substances is a normal part of being a teenager. The occasional party at a friend's house will always have alcohol and drugs present. When you were a teenager, I'm sure you must have also experimented with these substances at least once. However, regular use of these substances can lead to a more serious problem. Teenagers who have become addicted or dependent on drugs and alcohol will almost always display signs of anger and rebellion. Whenever their parents try to talk to them about staying clear of these substances, they may immediately become defensive and lash out.

How Does Substance Abuse Fuel Rebellion

Continuous use of drugs and alcohol can lead to personality disorders among teenagers. Being under the influence of their friends, teenagers can become rebellious and fearless. When they don't have access to drugs and alcohol, they may become frustrated and temperamental. You will notice behavioral changes in your teen that are violent and aggressive whenever they are not under the influence of drugs and/or alcohol. There are thousands of teenagers who have completely changed their personalities after becoming involved with these substances. They can go from being a loving, caring, and outgoing teenager, to being impulsive, angry, and withdrawn. Substance abuse has the power to completely change your teenager's life for the worse. It can leave permanent scars that will always haunt them if they don't take care of the problem early on, before it gets out of hand. Parents should not underestimate their teenager's use of drugs and alcohol, because once your teenager notices that you are okay with it, they may go all out without any limits.

Why Do Teenagers Become Involved With Substances?

A teenager's mind is a mess. There are so many things happening all at once to them. Physical changes, emotional changes, the pressures of excelling at school, and the pressures of being accepted into a social circle. Now add family problems, abuse, and other types of traumatic issues into that whole mix. All a teenager wants is to escape from their own thoughts and feelings, so they take refuge in these substances. When they are under the influence of drugs and alcohol, they don't feel unworthy or depressed. When they are around friends who engage in the same behavior, they feel accepted, like they belong there with them.

Your teenager could be involved with drugs and alcohol because of a number of reasons. It's best not to make any assumptions of your own when you are trying to find the root cause of their behavior. Sit down and have a talk with your teen about why they are seeking comfort in these substances. Instead of being angry and disappointed in them, try to be more supportive, so that you can get to the heart of the matter. Whether it's because of peer pressure, or because they are seeking an escape from reality, your teenager needs your help and guidance to overcome their addiction.

Reason 5: Mental Health Issues, Behavioral Disorders and Eating Disorders

Another reason why your teenager has turned rebellious may be because of mental health issues. Whether you are aware of them or not, mental health issues such as depression, anxiety, bipolar disorder, Attention Deficit Hyperactivity Disorder (ADHD), and many others often flare up during the teenage years. This flare up occurs because of the increased activity in the brain during the adolescent years. All the hormonal and physical changes tend to set off mental health issues in many teenagers, especially if they have been diagnosed with a mental health condition in their childhood. If your child has a pre-existing mental health condition, then you should consider this as a reason why your teen has become rebellious. Below, we will explore the different types of mental health issues teenagers can develop during adolescence.

Mental Health Disorders In Teenagers

It is estimated, globally, that every 1 in 7 (14%) of kids aged 10-19 will experience mental health conditions. Most of these cases go untreated because they aren't detected by parents or caregivers. (World Health Organization, 2021) Teenagers who have mental health issues tend to be excluded from social circles, and they are discriminated against by teachers. Teenagers are prone to developing mental health conditions, particularly during their adolescent years. There are also several other factors that contribute to this problem, such as poverty, abuse, and conflict within the home, as previously discussed. The more negative influences a teenager is exposed to, the greater the chance of them developing a mental health disorder.

However, in certain instances, teenagers are born with an existing mental health condition. When these issues are identified earlier on in childhood, parents have a better chance of getting them under control. There are certain instances where these mental health conditions go undetected in childhood, and they emerge during the adolescent phase. Even if teenagers have their mental illness under control, there will be times when it may get out of hand. Let's take a look at some common disorders teenagers experience during adolescence.

Emotional Disorders

It is estimated that 3.6% of teens aged 10-14 and 4.6% of teens aged 15-19 will develop an emotional disorder, such as anxiety (World Health Organization, 2021). Depression is also common among teenagers aged 15-18, and is brought upon by a number of factors. You are probably shocked at these statistics. Teenagers suffering from anxiety disorders and depression at such a young age seem almost impossible to understand. Parents sometimes question their teenagers' diagnosis because they are unable to grasp the fact that a teenager can experience depression when they have no bills to pay, no kids to support, and no pressures from working full-time jobs. Many parents don't have a basic understanding of how depression and anxiety disorders work.

Depression has a lot to do with the way your brain functions. There are certain chemicals in the brain which are responsible for regulating your emotions. When there is a problem with how these chemicals are released, it can lead to complications such as mood disorders and depression. The amygdala, the part of the brain responsible for regulating emotions, is where a lot of the work takes place. When there is a miscommunication with the signals being carried through the neurons, it can lead to chemically-induced depression. Your teenager goes through a lot of hormonal changes during adolescence, and the brain can malfunction because of an overload of the different hormones and chemicals being released. External factors, such as family conflict and substance abuse, can cause depression to become worse over time. This is where medication comes in, to help establish a good balance in the way neurons communicate with each other, thus creating order and a good flow of activity in the amygdala.

Parents need to gain an understanding of how depression works before they can pass judgment on their teenagers. Your teen also goes through stress and anxiety because of school, family issues, and their own personal problems. Be patient and understanding with them; that is all they need during this difficult phase. Most teenagers don't even understand what is going on with themselves. They have no idea that they might have depression or anxiety. All they know is that they feel unhappy, stressed out, anxious all the time, and unmotivated. To help them get through this, they engage in substance abuse. If parents paid more attention to their teenagers, they may notice these signs of mental illness. It is a parent's duty to help their teenager understand depression and anxiety, so that they can gain an understanding of how to help themselves.

Behavioral Disorders

Teenagers who fall under the younger category of ages 10-14 are more likely to develop behavioral disorders. ADHD is common among children in their early teen years. Teenagers who have ADHD find it hard to concentrate or pay attention for long periods of time. They are hyperactive and usually do things without thinking about the consequences, or how it will affect those around them. There is also another type of behavioral disorder that exists among teenagers, which is known as conduct disorder. The signs of this type of disorder include destructive behavior, disrespect, and aggressiveness. If you notice signs of behavioral disorders in your teenager, you have to take immediate action. If left ignored and untreated, your teenager could end up committing crimes as they grow older.

A lot of the anger your teenager has could be coming from places they don't understand. These mental health issues, such as behavioral disorders, cause a lot of anger and stress, which becomes too intense for your teenager to deal with on their own. When this happens, medication is typically prescribed by doctors to help your teenager cope with their emotions and behavior. Your teen might just be required to be on medication for a few years, until their adolescent phase has passed. In certain instances where there disorder has nothing to do with adolescence, they will be required to take the medication for the rest of their life. Parents should not feel ashamed of their kids if they struggle with mental health issues; these conditions are common among teenagers all around the world, and parents should not make their teenagers feel bad about their conditions, either. They can overcome these conditions with love and support from their parents, friends, and teachers. A teenager's emotional state could be even more fragile if they have any of these mental health problems that are common in puberty, so parents have to be extra diligent about what they say and do around their teenagers.

Risky Behavior

One thing that people notice about teenagers is that they are always ready to take a risk. They frequently display a "don't care" attitude that drives them to participate in activities that could be dangerous for them. The majority of people who are involved with drugs and alcohol will tell you that they started when they were teenagers. It always starts with that first puff of a cigarette, and ends with them being involved in all kinds of different drugs. Apart from substance abuse, there are other risk-taking behaviors, such as engaging in unprotected sex, stealing, and fighting. Teenagers are huge risk-takers because of their curiosity towards all these things that are labeled as "off limits" by their parents and teachers. They want to explore and find their own answers to their questions, without being influenced by the opinions of their parents. Because they don't have the ability or maturity to make good decisions at such a young age, they often rush into things without thinking about the end result.

The more their parents tell them no, the more they want to actually do it. So, parents should focus on teaching their children instead of instructing them. When they ask you questions about why they aren't allowed to engage in certain activities, be open and honest with them instead of shutting their questions down, because this causes them to rebel more. Apart from being curious, teenagers who suffer from mental health issues are more likely to rush into things without thinking. They look at drugs, alcohol, and sex as a type of comfort to the raging storm that is brewing within their mind. A depressed teenager won't really care about their own life, so they won't hold themselves back from getting involved with anything dangerous.

Eating Disorders

Eating disorders are common among teenagers, mostly girls, and it usually begins during adolescence. Anorexia nervosa and bulimia nervosa are the two most common eating disorders among teenage girls these days. One of the main signs that indicate your teenager could be suffering from an eating disorder is the rapid drop in their weight. Sometimes, parents might think that their teenager is starving themselves because they desire a slim figure so that they will be socially accepted. However, the majority of the time teenagers are unable to control their eating disorders because it has become a product of their mental health. In this case, their only hope of recovery would be through seeking professional help such as therapy.

During adolescence, teenagers will become increasingly paranoid about their outward appearance. They may find faults in themselves that don't really exist because of their low self-esteem issues. Seeing models in magazines or on social media and wanting a figure just like that is often the thought that starts the ball rolling with these eating disorders. Thinking that they're too fat or too curvy, and that they need to lose a drastic amount of weight in order to be accepted by their friends and family, is how a teenager who suffers from an eating disorder typically feels about themselves. In certain cases, teenagers don't have a limit to their weight loss, and they become so thin that it actually causes health conditions to emerge, such as low blood pressure, heart problems, and anemia.

How Does Anger Impact Parent-Teen Relationships

Living with an angry teenager can be anything but normal for many parents. One moment you're raising a cheerful, pleasant child, and the next moment you have a fire-breathing 15-year-old walking around the house, waiting to wreak havoc. Now, for those parents who haven't reached this stage yet with their kids, you may be thinking that we're being a bit dramatic. How bad could a teenager's anger get? They are just kids, after all, so what could possibly be so bad about it? Trust me when I say, no parent is prepared for the horror that they face with their teenagers. There are parents who have claimed to walk on eggshells because they try to avoid a confrontation with their angry teenager. Teenage anger can have a negative impact on a teen's life, from their relationships with their loved ones to their school and social lives.

Anger and How It Affects Family Relationships

Relationships are necessary in life. Whether we like it or not, our entire lives revolve around relationships. A teenager will share relationships with different people in their lives, such as their parents or caregivers, siblings, aunts and uncles, and their grandparents. At school, they will share relationships with their friends and teachers, and in their neighborhood, they will share relationships with the people they see daily. In order to maintain relationships, you have to be respectful, helpful, and genuine, and being an angry teenager can cause plenty of issues in their relationships with other people. Anger is a powerful emotion that can instantly bring division among the closest people, and the damage it causes can last a lifetime. For a teenager, anger can be all-consuming, because they don't have the ability to self-regulate their emotions. Letting their anger get the best of them is a common trait many teenagers have, and this can ruin relationships between family and friends. When a parent is dealing with a teenager who is rebellious, angry, aggressive, and disrespectful, it can be a nightmare that never ends. The disrespect and disregard a teenager has for their parents and siblings can hurt a lot and cause many relationships to become strained.

Parents begin to lose touch with their teenagers because they feel like there is going to be a problem whenever they try to talk to them. It can be depressing and stressful for parents to feel like they don't know who their teenager has become. The strained relationship makes room for further misunderstandings to crop up between parent and child. Your teenager may begin to feel judged and unloved by you, not realizing that you are also feeling hurt and scared to speak to them about the situation. Other people in the family may also stay clear of your teenager, because they don't want to get on the bad side of your teen. Most family members pull away when they feel disrespected, so the more anger your teen displays, the more damage will spread among their relationships with family members.

Teenagers need their parents by their side during their adolescent years. This can be a confusing time when parental guidance is most needed. However, because of anger, many teenagers feel as if no one understands them, so they push their parents and other family members away. When their parents give them advice or try to correct their behavior, they feel attacked, and retaliate with harsh words and sometimes even violence. There are thousands of teenagers who are homeless today because their parents kicked them out of their home. These parents had no idea how to approach the situation, or what was needed to help their teenagers change. They let anger and frustration get the best of them, and they decided not to put up with their troubled teenagers any longer, kicking them out to fend for themselves.

When parents don't know how to handle an angry teenager, they could do something that might end up ruining the lives of their children. Acting out of anger and hurt instead of parental instinct and love could destroy the relationship parents share with their teenagers. And when teenagers don't know when to draw the line, they also cause lifelong damage to their relationships. Parents must learn how to deal with their angry teenagers in a healthy way that will promote a good relationship between them, leaving no room for misunderstandings.

Teenage Anger and Its Impact on School Life

A teenager spends a lot of their time at school, around their friends and teachers. They have to be on their best behavior, and their mindset has to be focused on their work. This can become difficult for teenagers who develop a problem with their anger. Keeping their emotions in check, especially when around other teenagers who are mean to them, must be very difficult. This is why there are so many fights in high school among teenagers. An angry teenager is usually compared to a walking time bomb: you never know when they will explode. Although many teenagers hate going to school, it is a very important part of their lives, and it cannot be jeopardized under any circumstance. This is where a teenager learns a lot of critical things about themselves; for example, creating a sense of independence, making friends, learning about the world, and setting the foundation for the rest of their lives.

Anger can ruin all this in a split second. All it takes is a single moment; one bad decision fueled by anger. Teenagers being expelled from school over bad conduct isn't a rare occurrence, especially when it has to do with getting involved in fights. In certain instances where teenagers are expelled, they will refuse to continue with their education, so they drop out of school. Without completing their education, they don't have any foundation to build a future on. They lose all the friends they once had, and they become depressed as a result of that.

How Does This Anger Impact Their Personal Lives?

Because adolescence is an emotional time for teenagers where they feel everything on a deeper level, anger is one of those emotions which becomes hard to control. No one likes to feel angry, it isn't a positive emotion that brings you joy or peace. Instead, it keeps you on edge and consumes your entire being to the point where you no longer recognize yourself. A teenager is in the phase of life where they are learning about themselves. If they are constantly angry, they adapt to this, and make it a part of their personality. If they don't learn how to deal with their anger in a healthy way, it will become bottled up inside of them. That pent-up anger can remain dormant for a number of years, until such a time when it can no longer remain contained. Depending on where you are in life, if that anger breaks free, it can ruin you emotionally and mentally.

Imagine waking up every morning feeling angry at the world. The only thing you can focus on is being angry, and you miss out on enjoying your life. You don't notice the beautiful sunrise every morning, or the joy of having your family eat breakfast with you at the table. You let all of these moments go by because you are so consumed by anger. How would this make you feel? If this can be unbearable to think about as an adult, can you imagine what a teenager might be going through? A 14 year old with no ability to self-regulate their anger, waking up and feeling this way without understanding why, and not knowing what to do to help themselves deal with it. Then, if they go to school and get picked on by other kids, they become even more angry. The cycle perpetuates.

Further, if they then come home and hear the angry voices of their parents fighting or nagging at them, it only adds to that anger they have already been building up inside them. They are bound to explode sooner than later, and when they do, it's only going to make things more complicated. If they don't have anyone to help them through their anger, they will be forced to develop their own coping mechanisms, which usually involve substance abuse and violence. These teenagers will be destroying their own lives, and all because of emotions they don't understand or have help to deal with.

Chapter 3:
Warning! Your Teenager Is in Trouble

Signs That Indicate Your Teenager Is Headed Down the Wrong Road

Raising a teenager is no walk in the park. No matter how much you do for them, it always seems like it just isn't enough. The endless hours you put in working to support them, slogging all day cooking healthy meals, making sure they have clean clothing to wear, helping them with their homework, and nursing them back to health when they are sick. Being a parent is a full-time job. You don't get any breaks or vacations, and the best part is you don't even get paid for the overtime hours you put in. A parent only gets rewarded when they see what a great human being they have raised. A child who is responsible, respectful, hardworking, and joyful; that is all a parent ever wants. However, this can be a complete dream for many parents today. Teenagers are far from what their parents always dreamed of. In fact, they are completely the opposite. And it isn't because they choose to be this way. That's just how teenagers are.

But there can be instances where your teenager might be headed for trouble, and this is where a parent comes in and steers them in the right direction, before it's too late. Most parents won't be aware of any signs that their teenager is troubled, because teenagers are good at hiding their feelings. So, we have highlighted some signs you should keep an eye out for below. If you notice any of these signs in your teenager, then you need to start taking action as soon as possible.

Sign 1: Drastic Changes in Their Academic Performance

One of the first major signs that a parent notices about their troubled teenager is a drastic drop in their performance at school. There are teenagers who used to be bright students, who got straight As and always worked extra hard on their assignments and school projects. But now, suddenly, their results have started to fluctuate, because they are not showing any interest in their work. Now, there could be many reasons for their lack of motivation to perform better and strive for excellent marks, but when you notice that their whole attitude and demeanor changes as well, then you know that there's something deeper going on. We all understand that the workload gets tougher as the grades get higher; the same work you did when you were in fifth grade is not as difficult as the work put into the sixth grade. When your teenager enters high school, they might not be prepared for the different kinds of work that is being taught at these higher grades. It may become difficult to understand and keep up with the work. So instead of trying harder, many teenagers may choose to ignore their work because they don't feel confident in themselves anymore.

The moment your teenager stops displaying interest in their school work is when parents should start asking questions and stop ignoring their teenager's behavior. It's normal to expect your teenager to slip up once in a while; even they become pressured and stressed about their school work. But when there is a rapid decline with no sign of improvement, then your teenager is headed for trouble. Academic success is an important factor that should not be overlooked. There are a number of reasons why your teenager loses interest in their academic work, but parents have to understand if the problem is severe or not. We will explore more about this topic further along in the book.

Sign 2: Isolating Themselves and Losing Interest In Their Hobbies

It isn't uncommon for teenagers to want to lock themselves up in their rooms all day without talking to any of their family members. As they become older, privacy becomes a significant factor for many teenagers. The alone time helps them deal with their own issues and enables them to find ways to cope with their feelings. However, if your teenager is usually the talkative type who likes to hang out with people, then isolating themselves could point to a potential concern. If you notice your teenager becoming withdrawn from doing the things they normally would, like going out with family or friends, or missing out on attending extracurricular activities like swim class, then there could be something sinister going on. No one knows their child better than a parent does, so you will notice when your teenager is being stubborn or arrogant and just throwing a tantrum, or whether they are really losing interest in the things they used to love doing.

A teenager would only lose interest in their hobbies if something traumatic or disturbing has happened to them. Why else would you give up on something that brings you happiness and joy? Yes, people lose interest in their hobbies after a while; there is nothing uncommon about that. However, they gradually ease out of these hobbies over a period of time, they don't just stop doing them suddenly. This should be a cause for concern for parents because it could indicate that their teenager has experienced something horrible which needs to be addressed immediately. Unfortunately, many parents fail to pay attention to their teenagers, so they are unable to see any of these signs for themselves.

Sign 3: Being Disrespectful and Hurtful Towards Others

There will be rebellious moments when your teenager displays behavior that is disrespectful towards their parents, siblings, or teachers. The emotional and physical changes that they are experiencing can be hard to control sometimes, so they might just lash out suddenly without warning, and quickly correct their behavior shortly after realizing what they've done. However, if your teenager has been catching an attitude on a regular basis, where being disrespectful is something that is now second nature to them, then there could be something going on with your teenager. Rebellious teenagers who are constantly being disrespectful, their behavior is typically driven by something that is upsetting them. They could be using disrespect as a way of putting a wall up around themselves to keep others out. Parents should pay close attention to the behavior of their teenagers, because things are not always as they seem.

There are a few questions you should ask yourself about your teenager. Are they being disrespectful to everyone they meet, or only towards certain people? Has there been any major life changes recently that could have caused the change in behavior? Is my teenager doing okay in other areas of their life? These questions can help you see the bigger picture, and it will prevent you from making any assumptions without understanding your child first. Nowadays, parents are quick to judge their teenagers without getting to the bottom of things first, which can worsen the situation.

Sign 4: Lack of Drive and Ambition to Pursue Their Dreams

This is another major sign that your teenager is headed down the wrong road. People succeed only because of their own personal drive and ambition. When you want something badly enough, you will do whatever it takes to get it. A lack of ambition or drive can be a sign of depression in your teenager. At this ripe young age, your teenager should have so many dreams that they want to achieve. The world is their oyster, and they can do anything they set their minds to. You will hear teenagers talking about their futures all of the time, boasting among friends about the kind of car they're going to drive, or the amount of money they're going to make. If your teen is engaging in these conversations, then that is a good sign that they are on the straight path to success.

As a parent, if you've ever sat down with your teenager and asked them about their dreams and aspirations, and all you ever heard them say was "I don't know," then you need to be concerned. Usually teenagers aged 14-16 won't really have a clear picture of what their goals and ambitions are, so you shouldn't be too concerned then. But if your teenager is aged 17-19, and they still have no clue about their future, then this could point to a real problem. If your teenager is involved with drugs and alcohol, they most definitely won't be interested in what the future holds for them.

Sign 5: Bullying Other Kids

Bullies prey on weaker kids who they can take advantage of to make themselves feel better about something that is affecting them personally. If you have noticed certain traits in your teenager that are similar to those present in a bully, then it could very well mean that your teenager has been bullying other kids. There are certain signs that you should keep an eye out for that will help you identify whether your teenager is a bully. Is your teenager having problems with their sleep? Are they getting into trouble more often at school? Do you notice the manner in which they engage with others? Are other teenagers scared to be around them? Do they have a self-entitled attitude? If you have answered yes to any of these questions, then that means your teenager could be a bully.

It might seem as if your teenager enjoys being a bully because they feel good about hurting others, but realistically, there is something very wrong going on inside of them. They have been through some type of trauma or pain that has led them to take on this horrible role. Remember, teenagers don't understand how to control their feelings. They are not aware of what it takes to deal with negative emotions properly, without causing harm to others. Because of their ignorance and immaturity, they start inflicting pain upon those that are weaker than they are. This gives them a sense of control over one aspect of their lives, when everything else seems to be falling apart. If your teenager is a bully, you should seek professional help for them as soon as you can.

Sign 6: *Neglecting Their Personal Hygiene*

Teenagers are generally lazy in nature, especially when it comes to their personal hygiene and neatness. They dress in baggy sweatpants, t-shirts, and vests, and they don't really care about combing their hair or tying their shoe laces. This is how teenagers are, young and carefree, unbothered about things that don't appease them. However, you do come across certain teenagers who do take pride in their dressing and overall hygiene. Parents notice these things about their kids, so if you have a teenager who does practice good hygiene and takes pride in their dressing, seeing them turn into the complete opposite would have you scratching your head, wondering what went wrong. When your teenager stops showering daily, clipping their nails, or dressing in clean clothing, it can indicate that they are going through issues that are consuming their time and focus.

Teenagers who are severely depressed or under the influence of substances may lose all regard toward their personal hygiene. A lack of motivation to wake up every day and bathe, dress properly, comb their hair, make their beds, and clean their rooms, is what causes teenagers to lose their focus. Put yourself in their shoes for a few minutes. If your mind was a mess, all of these different thoughts and emotions floating around, taking up enormous amounts of your mental energy and space, would you be able to keep yourself neat and tidy? Would you have the ability to take care of yourself the way you were supposed to, being in the state of distress that you're in? Your answer would most likely be a huge "no!" If you cannot first take care of yourself, there is no way that you can ever take care of the surrounding responsibilities in your life, like your home, your car, or your own physical body. If your teenager has reached this stage, then they most likely need to be taken in for therapy to help them overcome the troubles of their childhood and present days.

Sign 7: Self-Injury

Self-injury occurs when a person causes physical harm to themselves because of undergoing emotional trauma that they find hard to cope with. This is common among teenagers who suffer from depression and anxiety disorders. They cut themselves in the hopes of trying to relieve some of their emotional stress and frustration. Most of them cut on their arms, thighs, or any other part of their body that isn't easily visible to people. They will dress themselves in baggy clothing, such as hoodies, jeans, and sweatpants, even when it's hot outside, to cover up their scars. And they become withdrawn, always avoiding contact with people, and they don't like speaking too much about themselves. Teenagers who are involved with self-injury are in dire need of professional help.

Parents who suspect that their teenager has been cutting themselves should not turn a blind eye or avoid talking to them about it. Your teenager is desperately crying out for help. It's obvious that they cannot cope on their own. They don't know how to open up about their feelings, or share their experiences with you, so they choose to hurt themselves as a way of coping with their fears and trauma. This type of behavior is very dangerous; one cut too deep could end your teenager's life. Even though they aren't looking to end their lives, if they make one mistake, it could be the end for them. Parents have to be more in tune with their teenagers so that they don't miss any of the signs. You only have one chance to save your teenager, and it's worth the effort.

Sign 8: Emotional Outbursts

Have you ever tried to have a conversation with your teenager about something important, but every time you try, they become angry and slam their room door in your face? This isn't surprising behavior for teenagers. However, when they do this all of the time, it can indicate that there is something else going on with them emotionally. This sign is a hard one to miss, since it involves your teenager displaying behavior that is unstable. We all have our emotional outbursts from time to time. However, when it comes to a troubled teen, their outbursts could occur daily. There can be several reasons why your teenager might be crying all of the time, or lashing out during simple conversations. Depression, substance abuse, mental health disorders; these are just a few examples of what could cause the emotional outbursts, and all are very serious reasons that need to be addressed.

We can understand that it is hard for parents to deal with teenagers who are emotionally unstable. It can be draining and frustrating, to say the least, and most parents tend to throw in the towel sooner than later. However, holding on to your teenager and being persistent to help them change is the best thing a parent can do for their child. Remember, your teenager isn't behaving this way because they want to. They are finding it difficult to cope with their emotions. It's like they are experiencing an emotional overload and the only way to take off some pressure is by letting their emotions out all at once. This isn't a healthy way of coping with their emotions, so parents should help their teenagers find positive ways to de-stress and let go of the frustration. If left to continue on this path that they're on, they can become emotionally unstable people in the future, which can jeopardize their career, relationships, and overall success in life.

Sign 9: Stealing

Stealing is a big sign that your teenager might be up to no good. If you've been noticing things getting lost or disappearing more often, and when you ask your teenager about it, all they do is make up excuses, then it could mean that your teenager has been stealing these items. The iPad you bought your teenager for Christmas is now missing after two months and the new pair of Jordan's you bought for yourself are nowhere to be found after your teenager had borrowed them for their casual day at school. And, the 18-carat gold earrings your husband gave you for your anniversary have disappeared from your jewelry box, which your teenager always has access to. Does any of this sound familiar to you? If it does, then you could be dealing with a huge problem.

When teenagers start stealing, there could be several reasons behind it. Most of the time these reasons stem from substance abuse; being involved with drugs and alcohol. Or, it can stem from your teenager being pressured by outside influences, such as bad friends. If your teenager is stealing to support their own bad habits, it could indicate that they are very far gone into their addiction. Not knowing where to draw the line and doing things that are completely out of their personality shows just how badly they are being impacted by their outside influences, and also by their addiction. If parents don't take action against their teenagers as soon as they find out about their stealing, it can end up getting them locked up and thrown behind bars at a young age. No parent would want to see their child throw away their life, so when action is needed, parents should not back down.

Sign 10: Promiscuous Behavior

During adolescence, teenagers become increasingly curious about sex. They want to experiment and to see what the hype is all about. Most of the time they take sex advice from their friends, rather than from their parents. Sex can be an uncomfortable topic to talk about with parents, so teenagers avoid the "sex talk" at all costs, because no teenager will want to hear about the birds and the bees. However, as uncomfortable as the topic is, it still has to be discussed with your teenager at the right time. It's good to teach your teen about sex and how to stay protected against different diseases that are spread during sexual intercourse. Teenagers who don't understand what safe sex means usually take matters into their own hands to explore and learn as much as they can. Some teenagers use sex in the wrong way, and this can be dangerous for them.

If you notice that your teenager is being sexually active frequently, and that they have multiple sexual partners, it's time to sit down and have a talk with them. Engaging in promiscuous behavior at a young age can open all kinds of doors that can jeopardize your teenager's life. From contracting Sexually Transmitted Diseases (STD's) to getting pregnant at a young age, the consequences are too high for a teenager to bear. Typically, when teenagers are promiscuous, they are trying to use sex to comfort themselves or to help them cope with their emotions. Parents should help their teenagers understand the meaning of sex and how to practice safely whilst being sexually active.

These are just a few of the signs that indicate your teenager is headed for trouble. Parents should be able to tell the difference in their teenager's behavior. Sometimes, it can be very hard to tell what your teen might be thinking or doing. Teenagers are pros at hiding their emotions and wrongdoings from their parents and teachers. They will tell you exactly what you want to hear, without hesitating. That is why so many parents out there have no clue what their teenager is feeling, or what type of activities they are engaged in. Don't feel guilty if you have missed any of these signs in your teenager. Chances are, they have done a great job at hiding things from you. Now that you are aware of the signs, be on the lookout, and don't hesitate to call your teenager out for their behavior. Yes, they might hate you now, but they will be thankful later on in their lives.

Chapter 4:
When Technology Helps Your Teen Become Rebellious

Technology and Teenagers

There is no denying that advancements in technology have taken our world to new heights. We are able to do so much because of our "smart" devices, things that we never thought were possible a few years ago. Video calling, instant messaging, creating videos, and connecting with people from all over the world. All of these amazing features can come from one small device: a smartphone. Teenagers and tech go hand in hand. The world of technology is so appealing to teenagers, it's how they spend their every waking moment. From watching TV until late at night, to chatting with their friends on social media, to posting their daily activities online, a teenager simply cannot function without their smart devices. In this chapter, we take a look at how technology impacts a developing teenager, and we weigh the pros and cons of this remarkable invention.

Why Are Teenagers So Addicted to Technology?

Back in our day, we spent the majority of our time hanging out with our friends at the bioscope, wandering into forbidden places, and skipping school to laze around all day at our friends' houses. There was no such thing as mobile phones or smart TV's to captivate our attention. If we wanted to be entertained, we would play games at the arcade or watch other kids play hopscotch in the park. Nowadays, teenagers don't even know what hopscotch is. They are too busy learning how to post updates on their social media platforms. They have missed out on the experience of living, and they don't know what it's like to socialize face to face with others. They haven't climbed trees or scraped up their knees whilst learning how to ride a bike for the first time, and if they want to play a game, they do it on their smartphones or laptops. Basically, they don't know what it's like being a real teenager because they are always hiding behind their phones.

Why Do Teenagers Use Technology?

There are many reasons why a teenager chooses to use technology instead of getting things done the old-fashioned way. One of the main reasons is that it is more convenient to communicate with someone over the phone than it is to spend time with them physically. Teenagers are easily influenced by what is happening around them. They pick up on the latest trends in fashion and technology, and they ensure that they never miss out on the latest gossip. All of this is made possible through the wonderful invention called the smartphone. They can do everything from the comfort of their own homes: watch the latest movies, play video games online with their friends, browse through social media to stay updated with what their friends are doing, and even complete assignments and research projects, all from their hand held devices.

Technology isn't all that bad. There are some advantages for teenagers that help make their lives a bit easier. The internet and the smartphone, together, are unbeatable when it comes to getting things done faster. Back in the day, if we had to do some research on a topic for a school assignment, we would go to the local library and look up books and magazine articles to get information. Now, all you have to do is type your search topic on the internet and hit the search button. All the information you need is displayed right there, at your fingertips. How amazing is that? I bet if you were a teenager in today's world, you would be fascinated with technology as well. During the COVID-19 pandemic, teenagers could study from home through their smartphones and laptops, and they didn't even have to attend school to write their tests. Everything was completed online, whilst their teachers were monitoring their answers live. Technology is our future, so our teenagers have to be clued-up with applying it to their everyday lives.

How Does Technology Impact the Human Brain?

Technology use has increased drastically over the past few years. A whopping 95% of teenagers in the U.S. have access to a smartphone, and 45% of them have claimed that they're constantly online throughout the day (Cross, 2019). This is a huge amount of time being spent on a screen, especially for teenagers, whose brains are still developing and growing. With the noticeable increase of technology use among teenagers, the suicide rate has also increased proportionately over the last few years. However, with the rates of depression among teenagers rising along with the use of technology, there is no hard evidence to show that there is a possible connection between the two. If you had to sit down and try to have a conversation with a teenager, you would be surprised as to how long they can do so without glancing down at their phone. No more than a few minutes into the conversation would their attention be shifted onto their smart device.

This shows a pattern of addiction that exists between a teenager and their smartphone. It is an unhealthy habit to constantly be on their phones, scrolling through their apps, and feeding into their need to be entertained all of the time. Itcan impact their brain negatively. Teenagers have admitted to feeling addicted to their phone. Whenever they receive a notification, they immediately feel the urge to leave whatever they are doing and respond. This incessant use of their smartphones causes decreased brain connectivity and promotes self-isolation. The world that exists within a smartphone appeals to a teenager as the ideal world in which they would rather spend their time. Troubled teenagers, who have issues with family conflict, often turn to their smartphones for comfort because it helps them escape the harsh reality that they are living in. Others are addicted to the games and social media apps because it opens up a world of entertainment which is literally right at their fingertips. Irrespective of what the reasons could be, there is no way that excessive technology use can be justified.

A study about how children's brains responded to excessive use of technology was carried out by the National Institute of Health (NIH) back in 2018. They found that children and adolescent teenagers who spend more than two hours on their phones each day scored low on thinking and language tests. Those children and teens who spent more than seven hours a day on their phones started experiencing thinning of the cortex in the brain, the area responsible for reasoning, judgment, and critical thinking. (Cross, 2019) These smartphones impair their ability to learn and develop as a normal teenager would, because it takes away their opportunity to gain critical skills from engaging in real world situations. They will not be able to find solutions to real world problems, they won't understand how to interact with people, and they will lose confidence in themselves when they are forced to operate in the real world.

Every human being learns from their experiences as they grow older. Whatever we learn, we use to our advantage to bring us success in our careers and in our personal lives. These are skills we gained from going out and watching people, engaging with them, and learning from them. The bonds we built with our family members were strengthened by spending time with them and learning about one another. Our expertise in our fields of interest came from being involved in the process and paying attention to the mistakes that were made so that we could learn from them. If we were occupied with our smartphones back then, whilst we were growing up, do you think we would have been the same people we are today? Would you have the same knowledge and skills that you have today? I guess not, so how can we expect our teenagers to grow and develop into people who are better than us when we are allowing them to spend all of their precious time in front of a screen?

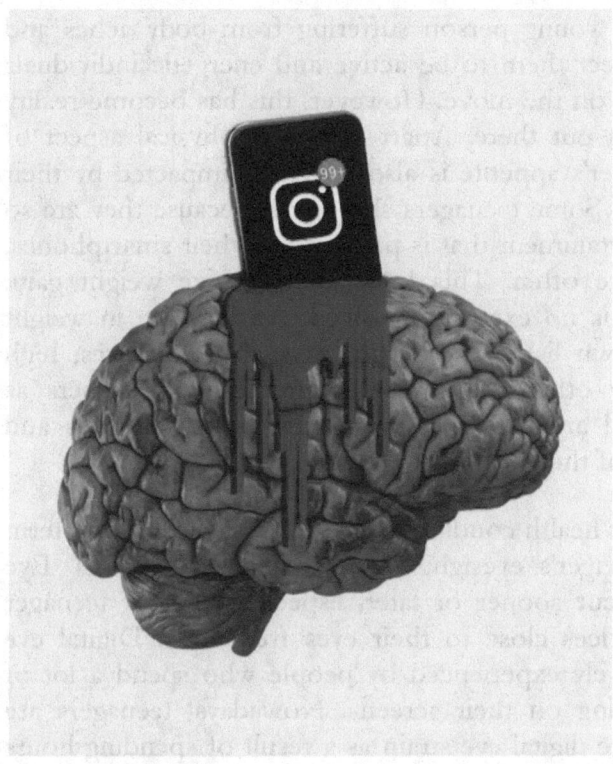

How Does Technology Impact the Physical Health of Your Teenager?

During adolescence, your teenager is still growing and developing. Their bodies have not yet fully developed, and they need to keep themselves healthy and active. How do they do this? Well, one thing is for sure, sitting in front of the TV or spending 90% of their time on their cell phones isn't going to help them stay fit. A teenager unknowingly jeopardizes their health by allowing technology to take over their lives. Instead of spending their time playing sports and being active, they lay in bed, giving all of their attention to their smart devices. This lack of physical activity affects your teenager's developing muscles and causes them to become weaker instead of stronger. By the time your teenager is around 20 years old, they will start developing issues with joint and muscle pain.

It's hard to imagine a young person suffering from body aches and pains. You would expect them to be active and energetic individuals who are living life and on the move. However, this has become reality for so many teenagers out there. Apart from the physical aspect of development, a teenager's appetite is also adversely impacted by their overuse of technology. Some teenagers skip meals because they are so consumed by the entertainment that is provided by their smartphones, whilst others eat more often. This leads to excessive weight gain, especially when there is no exercise involved. An increase in weight also comes with its own list of health issues such as diabetes, high cholesterol, and many other weight-related problems. Teenagers as young as 13 years old are being diagnosed with cardiac issues and hypertension because of their unhealthy lifestyle.

There are several other health conditions that can arise from long-term screen use. Your teenager's eyesight is one of these concerns. Eye strain is bound to occur sooner or later, especially if your teenager holds these smart devices close to their eyes frequently. Digital eye strain has become largely experienced by people who spend a lot of time reading or working on their screens. Nowadays, teenagers are beginning to experience digital eye strain as a result of spending hours on their tablets and smartphones. Eye strain causes blurred vision and dry eyes. Pain is experienced in the neck, around the shoulders, and is often accompanied by headaches.

Social Media and Its Connection to Teenage Rebellion

There's no doubt that social media has radically changed our world. People have accomplished so much through their use of social media. One of its biggest advantages is boosting sales for businesses both big and small. When used correctly, social media has the power to transform the lives of people all around the world. However, as incredible as it can be, social media also has the ability to destroy people's lives. You see, people are easily influenced by what they see on social media, with teenagers being on top of the list. It is the ultimate digital playground for teenagers, where everything is possible. Teens use their social media platforms to stay connected to their friends, to follow the lives of celebrities, to promote their talents and good looks, and to wreak havoc on other teenagers. Let's take a closer look at how social media plays a part in creating rebellious teenagers.

How are Teenagers Influenced by Social Media?

Teenagers are very impressionable individuals, who are easily influenced by things that catch their attention. Fashion, cars, food, beauty, money, alcohol, tattoos, and music, these are all of the things that a teenager will find most interesting during this phase in their lives. And guess what! Social media has all of this and more. There are several kinds of social media apps available that have their own special way of attracting teenagers to their platform. The influence that these platforms have over the youth is astounding. Your teenager can change their personality overnight, just from being exposed to something on social media. Teenagers have admitted to being negatively impacted by social media. It is claimed that 45% of teenagers felt overwhelmed by the drama that they see online, 43% of teens felt pressured to keep up appearances online, and 37% were stressed and anxious about how many likes and views their posts got (Cross, 2019).

These numbers speak for themselves: Teenagers are heavily influenced by social media. Sadly, this is also where teenage rebellion stems from. Teenagers always want to be like the people they see on social media. They want to be cool and popular, and sometimes they are willing to do anything to achieve this, even if it means going against the rules. Their persistence and insistence to be exactly like other teenagers or celebrities on social media blinds them from facing their own reality. Parents struggle with their stubborn teenagers who refuse to understand why there are rules in place. Teenagers become rebellious when things don't go their way; for instance, they want a new pair of expensive shoes that they've seen someone wear on social media. This person gained many "likes" because of this expensive pair of shoes, and so this teenager wants to do the same thing. However, their parents cannot afford to buy these shoes, so they offer to buy something similar, but less expensive. The teenager doesn't accept, and becomes angry and disrespectful.

Many parents will understand the example mentioned above. You expect your teenager to understand your position, however, they cannot do this because they are under the influence of these popular social media influencers. There is a reason why they're called "influencers," and it's because they have the power to coerce your teenager into doing whatever they see online, whether it's purchasing a new make-up pallet or participating in one of those social media challenges that are dangerous and stupid. You would be shocked as to how easily your teenager becomes influenced to do things that are completely different from their personality and their values. A parent will notice the sudden change in their teenager's behavior, but they often don't understand what could have contributed to this change. Your teenager becomes nothing but a puppet when they are spending so much of their time on these apps. They lose their own beliefs and fall for whatever they see on social media. It makes them feel entitled, and like they should also be living the kind of life that they see other teenagers living on these platforms.

Teenagers take quick notice of the expensive clothes and the parties, the lifestyles of the rich and famous, and they blindly start to desire these things for themselves. They don't take their parents' financial situations, religious beliefs, or social standing into consideration when they are making demands and going behind their parent's backs. Parents should understand that teenagers are unpredictable people; one minute you think you've got them all figured out, and the next minute they are someone completely different.

The Pros and Cons of Teenage Social Media Use

The only way parents can control their teenager's use of social media is if they have a clear understanding of what the pros and cons are. Social media can be beneficial when used in the right way, and parents can use this to their advantage. Let's explore the pros and cons of teenage social media use.

Pro—Good For Their Education

Social media provides a large pool of professionals who offer free advice on several aspects of education. Teenagers can access these social media pages and gather valuable information for their school projects and assignments. Resources can be limited at schools, and teachers don't always have the best sources of information to give to their students. The majority of the time, teenagers research information online, which is also a cost-effective way of getting their work completed.

Con—It's Addictive

It's no secret that social media can be addictive. Even adults can't fall asleep at night without scrolling through social media first. Teenagers are no different; they also become addicted to being online at all times. Whether they're in bed, at the table having breakfast, or even whilst using the toilet, teenagers are always on their phones. Addiction to social media is fairly new, so it can be hard to determine just how much it can impact a teenager's life. However, there are obvious signs which indicate that their addiction to social media is impacting their lives negatively.

Pro—Teenagers Pick Up New Skills

Your teenager can potentially learn a lot during their time on social media. There are so many ways to learn about new skills and hobbies which are displayed there. Step-by-step tutorials on nail application, make-up, building things, and cooking; these are available on various social media platforms. Back in the day, we didn't have any access to this type of technology. It wasn't so easy to learn new skills, so teenagers can benefit greatly from the advancements in technology today.

Con—Lose Touch With Reality

Teenagers who spend too much time on social media tend to lose touch with reality. They become so engrossed with the lives of others that they forget to live their own lives. They buy into this fake world that many influencers portray on social media, and they crave material things, completely forgetting about what they are blessed with in their own homes. These teenagers lose touch with their true selves, and take on a whole new persona that is appealing to the world of social media, but not to their own family and friends. This is a common issue that affects many teenagers, and likewise, adults.

Pro—Stay Connected to Friends and Family From Afar

Social media has made it possible for people to stay connected to their friends and family members who live far away from them, in other countries or states. Teenagers can maintain relationships with a parent after a divorce, or with their best friend they left behind when they moved to a new school. It brings people together and allows them to work as one team, even though they may be thousands of miles away from one another. This is one of the greatest advantages of social media.

Con—Cyberbullying

In this day and age bullying hasn't ceased to exist. Teenagers have now found a way to bully other kids online, through social media. This can be worse than bullying someone face to face, because teenagers are being publicly humiliated in front of thousands of people. Cyberbullying has severe consequences. It has become one of the main reasons why teenagers commit suicide. Most of the time, parents don't even have a clue that their teenager is being cyberbullied, so before parents can intervene, the damage has been done already.

Pro—It Promotes Creativity and Prepares Them For a Tech-Savvy Future

Our future has been taken over by technology. Day by day, everything is becoming more advanced, and the world is changing constantly. It can be challenging for people to adapt to these changes since they are so accustomed to getting things done a certain way. However, our teenagers are able to quickly adapt to change, all thanks to their involvement with social media. Here is where they learn about all new technology and how it's going to change their lives in the future. This innovation sparks creativity within these young minds. Teenagers can use this information to help them choose a wiser career path that will bring them success.

Parents, your teenagers have been exposed to this phenomenal world of social media—there's no taking that back. However, all hope is not lost. You can still guide your child down the right path. Show them that social media can be used differently, in a way that will help them grow and become better. Teach them about the world and how it works, and be honest with them about the dangers of social media. Don't leave them alone to figure things out just because they are being stubborn. Teenagers don't know what's good for them. They have no idea how the world works, and what kinds of people there are out there. Yes, you can let them find out on their own, but you should be there with them every step of the way to protect them and support them through it.

Your teenager's anger and "know it all" attitude might be too much for you to handle. But if you show them that you are bothered, they will hide more things from you out of fear of being judged and embarrassed. If they see that you are giving them their space to learn on their own, but are still there to support them, they will be more open and forthcoming with you about their experiences.

Chapter 5:
How You Can Help Your Teenager Through This Phase

Tips to Help You Become More Supportive and Understanding Towards Your teenager

A teenager is often described as someone who is misjudged, underestimated, lazy, and unbothered. But in reality, no one really understands what goes on inside a teenager's head (well, except for other teenagers). They are the only ones who can understand what another teenager is thinking. Even now, as an adult, if you had to sit back and reminisce about your days as a teenager, you would probably beat yourself up for all of the silly choices you've made back then. So, now when you try to understand your teenager, you won't be able to see things from their perspective because you no longer think like a teenager. Parents are likely to impose their own "adult-like" beliefs onto their teenagers, without realizing that their kids cannot see things their way because they are in the process of learning and developing their own ideals and beliefs.

Your teenager is learning how to become their own person. Interfering with that can cause a lot of damage to your teenager's self-confidence. In this chapter, we teach you how to help your teenager through their anger by being an understanding and supportive parent. Get ready to transform your parenting skills to create a better relationship with your child.

What Your Responsibilities Are as a Parent

These days, it can be very challenging to parent a teenager, especially with the opinions of other parents breathing down your neck. The new generation of parents have their own way of parenting their children. They believe in more freedom, more independence, and fewer rules for their teens to follow. This parenting style may work for some. However, every parent should develop their own parenting style that is tailored to the needs and behavior of their teenagers. There is no set manual that a parent should follow, although there are a few basic guidelines that have proven to be successful in parenting teenagers. Parents often don't know where to draw the line when it comes to parenting. There are certain aspects of your teenager's life that you are responsible for, and there are certain things that your teenager has to learn to cope with on their own. Below, we have listed these guidelines to help you gain a foundation by which you can start building a good parenting structure for your family.

Building a Strong Foundation

Since the day you found out that you were pregnant, your job as a parent began. You had to make sure that you ate healthy, rested well, took your prenatal vitamins, and kept yourself away from dangerous situations. The urge to protect your unborn baby was intense, and you made sure that you did everything it took to keep your baby safe. One of the most important tasks you have as a parent is to build a strong foundation for your child to grow up on. So what does it take to build a good foundation? It all starts the day you welcome your baby into the world. Making sure that your baby will be growing up in a safe environment where there is little to no crime or hazards around is one of the first things you do before taking your baby home.

Next, you ensure that your baby has everything they need: a crib, diapers, clothing, and formula. You spend your days raising your child with love, and you teach them right from wrong as they grow. Sending them to school and making sure that they get a good education is another significant aspect of building a solid foundation. Here, they will have a chance at a good future, no matter what your circumstances are. Your child's foundation starts at home, with their family, and with the way in which they are being raised. In certain instances, parents are unable to build a strong foundation for their children. There are several reasons for this:

- Parents don't have the finances to provide their children with a good home or with a good education.
- Parents have kids at a young age and are not mature enough to take good care of their children.
- Parents are involved with drugs and alcohol, which prevents them from being good parents to their children.
- Parents are abusive and violent towards their children, causing severe emotional and physical trauma.
- Parents fight among themselves. Constant conflict within the family, or an ugly divorce that is taking a toll on the children.

All of these issues mentioned above are just a few of the reasons why parents cannot build good foundations for their kids. If a child does not have good values and morals to build themselves on, they become troubled teenagers later on in life. When the foundation is shaky, it will not hold even in the toughest of situations. Your child would not be able to rebuild their lives on a weak foundation. If they ever want to restart their lives at any stage, they will have to build their own foundation from scratch. One that will help them withstand the storms of life. That is why, no matter how poor or rich you are, your job as a parent is to make sure that you instill good values and character in your child.

Make Hard Decisions for Their Own Good

Every single parent on this planet wants the best for their children. Sometimes, your job as a parent will include making decisions that are hard for your teenager to accept. It is well understood that teenagers have a mind of their own. They are free spirited, and they often do things on a whim. They don't tend to sit down and think about the decisions they make, so it's our job, as the parent, to make sure that we have a say in these decisions that our children are making. Parents must understand that as long as their teenager is under the age of 18 and living in their home, every decision that they make will include your input as well. There is a reason why the legal age for a teenager to become independent is 18 years old.

Before this age, your teenager does not have the maturity or wisdom to make decisions for themselves. Although they might be very confident in themselves, and they believe that they know what is best for them, a teenager will always need guidance from their parents, no matter how old they get. One of the main issues that arises between a parent and child is due to the fact that parents make decisions for their teenagers, which have to be accepted whether they like them or not. Have you ever said "no" to an overnight camping trip that your teenager wanted to go on with their friends? Are you aware of the reasons why you declined to let them go on this trip? Was your teenager happy about your decision? I guess the answer is obvious: your teenager was furious that they could not go along with their friends.

Parents always have a good reason when they choose to make decisions that their kids aren't happy with. No parent does anything out of spite or jealousy. If a parent says "no," it's because they only want their kids to be safe. There have been many situations where parents gave in to the demands of their teenagers, even though they knew in their heart of hearts that the decision they made was not right; andnd the consequences of that wrong decision led to their teenager losing their lives, or getting involved in something that would completely change their lives forever. Just one weak moment, one bad decision, could end up ruining your teenager's life. When a parent is making a decision, they must think about the best interest of their child first. There are several other factors that should be taken into consideration, such as the teenager's age, the type of friends they hang out with, whether the places they want to go to are safe and near home, or if their teenager is mature enough to handle any type of responsibility. Yes, your teenager's happiness is important; however, their safety comes first, always. They might not always agree with your decision, and they might even start to resent you for holding them back; but one day they will thank you for being there for them, even when they didn't realize just how much they needed you.

Teach Your Teenager About Being Independent

Independence is key to building a successful life for your teenager. The best thing any parent can do for their child is to teach them how to stand up on their own two feet. You see, this world has changed so much. It is tough out there, and people need to be equipped to handle the pressures that come from the world. The competition is fierce. There are millions of people who are all vying for the top, and they are doing whatever it takes to get there. How do you think a spoiled teenager, who relies on their parents to get things done for them, is going to survive in this cruel world? Truth be told, they wouldn't even last a day on their own. And this is sad because these teenagers are not to blame; it's their parents who need to be held accountable for making their teenagers this way.

As parents, we often make the mistake of giving our kids everything they want because we love them, and we want them to know this. There are parents who spoil their kids rotten by financing their every need, cleaning up after them, giving them permission to do whatever they want to do, and always taking their side, even when they are wrong. Sometimes, parents allow their love for their children to blind them to such an extent that they can't see the damage being done. Once your child reaches a certain age, 10 to 12 years old, you, as a parent, should be teaching your child how to start taking care of themselves. Teach them to make their beds, get their clothing ready for school, do the dishes after supper, and earn an allowance by making sure that these chores are done daily. You are not being mean or lazy when you are letting your kids work hard. You are teaching them invaluable lessons about life that they will need in the future.

We've all met those self-entitled teenagers who walk around like they own everybody else. Dressed in the latest designer fashion, chatting away on the latest smartphone, and driving the latest sports car that other people wish they could have. Haven't you ever stopped to wonder, what did these teenagers do to deserve such a lavish lifestyle? Well, they really didn't have to do anything, because their parents are very wealthy. Giving your child everything on a silver platter is the worst mistake any parent can make. I know these parents are probably thinking that their kids will never have to work because they will inherit all of the wealth from their parents, and go on to live a fabulous life. But in reality, when things fall apart (which they sometimes suddenly do), what would these teenagers do? How would they become independent without the help of their parents? Parents need to push their teenagers to work hard for their own fortune so that they can live independently one day. They should be able to clean their own homes, cook their own meals, and make their own money.

Make Sure That Your Child Takes Responsibility for Their Actions

Holding your child accountable whenever they make a mistake is another significant part of being a good parent. You should never allow your teenager to shirk their responsibilities or shift blame for something they did onto someone else. Taking account for their actions and accepting their faults whenever they do something wrong is an essential part of being an honest human being. Parents should never make excuses for their teenager's behavior or for their actions. When your teen messes up, allow them to face the music on their own. Parents who cover up for their children, especially when they have hurt someone else by their actions or words, are setting their teenagers up to have an infallible attitude and mindset about themselves.

This is how narcissistic people are created, and unfortunately it stems from being raised by parents who never teach them about being accountable for their actions. Because teenagers are so impressionable, they quickly develop an egotistical attitude about themselves, thinking that they are always right and never wrong. They are under the impression that if their parents believe that whatever they do is right, then the whole world should also feel the same way. This is the wrong way to live. Everyone makes mistakes, and everyone should own up to their mistakes. No one is perfect, and that is part of being human. Parents have to teach their children that it is okay to make mistakes; you are learning from them after all. However, you must also hold yourself accountable for these mistakes so that you can do better next time. As long as your teenager doesn't accept responsibility for their mistakes, they will never learn or grow into better versions of themselves.

Encourage, Motivate, and Empower

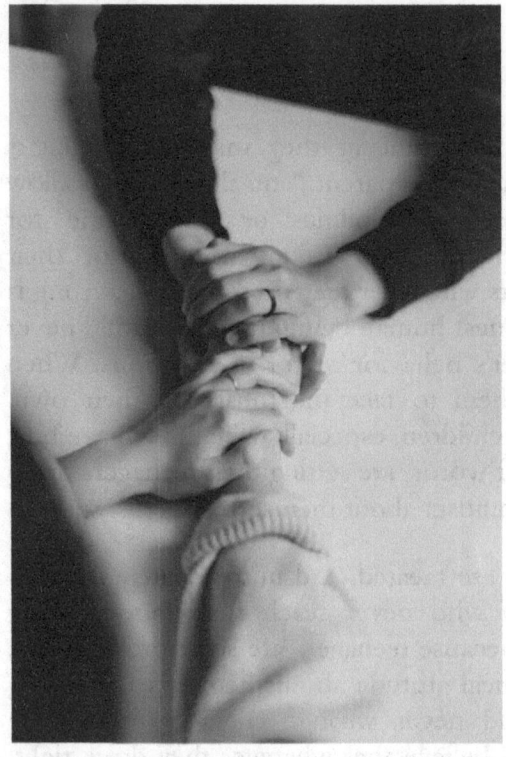

During this difficult time in their lives, a teenager will need as much love and support as they can get from their parents and family members. The most basic role of a parent is to nurture and empower their children to be the best that they can be. Whenever your teenager faces failure in their lives, you should be there to motivate them to try again and succeed. If your teenager is experiencing depression, or if they are unsure about their ability to face the hardships of life, you should empower them and encourage them to hold on. You must understand that your teenager isn't perfect. Don't compare your child to another. Each child is different in their own way. Parents can be quick to judge their teenagers without thinking about how it will affect them in the long run. Every time you shout at your teen, or say something mean in the heat of the moment, your teenager is being destroyed by your words and actions. Just because they are angry all of the time doesn't mean that they are being selfish, or that they are behaving this way on purpose. Teenagers want their parents to understand what they are feeling, and they want you to be patient with them, even when they are being difficult to handle. It isn't easy being a teenager, especially one that is troubled.

Most parents who don't try to understand what their teenager is going through become distant and judgmental towards their children. This only worsens the situation, causing their teenager to act out in ways that can potentially ruin their lives. All they really want to do is get back at their parents, so they become rebellious. They end up doing things intentionally and pressing all of the right buttons just to get their parents' attention. Once you can understand this about your teenager, then you will see things from their perspective. It's imperative that parents show their teenagers how much they love them, because your child will be questioning their self-worth constantly during adolescence. The last thing you would want is for your teenager to feel bad about themselves, so put aside your pride and be there to support them.

What You Should Avoid Doing as a Parent

As much as you want to be a great parent to your teenager, there are a few important things to remember. You cannot be the type of parent who is always breathing down your teenager's neck. Parenting isn't easy, and everyone knows that teenagers have a mind of their own. We often make mistakes, especially when we are first-time parents with zero experience or guidance. Sometimes, we can go a bit overboard and become paranoid over every little thing. There's nothing more a teenager hates than having an overbearing parent. Yes, teenagers have to be disciplined and monitored from time to time. However, there are certain things you should avoid doing as a parent. Below, we have created a list of what you should avoid doing to ensure that you are being the best parent you can be for your teenager.

Always Trying to Make Sure That Your Kids Are Happy

It's a given that we, as parents, always want our kids to be happy. We want to see them smiling, laughing, and enjoying life. But as much as we want nothing but happiness and joy for them, we also have to face reality. There will be happiness and dark times in our lives; that's just how it works. Your teenager is no different from any other human being on this planet. There will be times when they will get hurt, become angry, and feel unhappy. You have to accept this, because it's the only way you can really help your teenager. When you go out of your way to make sure that your child is happy, eventually they start expecting you to do everything they want. Whenever you deny them anything, they start becoming upset and angry. Being the parent that you are, who wants to always see your child happy, you give in to their demands just so that you don't feel guilty about saying no and upsetting your child. Most of the time, parents don't even realize that they are doing this, and they miss the fact that they are spoiling their teenager by always saying "yes."

This can have adverse effects on your teenager's life, causing them to develop a self-entitled attitude and mindset. When you are making a decision that is in the best interest of your child, you don't have to feel guilty or sad that your teenager doesn't agree with it. They are still too young to understand what is good for them, and they cannot see the bigger picture—but you can. Is your child's momentary happiness and satisfaction more important than their future and their safety? No. So take a stand and be confident in yourself when you are saying "no" to your teenager. You are their parent, not their bestie, so stop feeling guilty about making the right choices for them. Whether they like you or not, your job as a parent is to guide them down the right path, and you cannot do this if you are giving in to their every whim.

Worried About the Approval of Others

Parenting is not a competition, and even though so many parents try to outdo one another these days, the fact remains true. You do not need to gain the approval of anyone around you, and you should not be parenting your child as if you are participating in a contest, either. Let's be realistic; there is no trophy or reward that you are going to achieve just because you do everything by the book. Your reward lies with the wellbeing of your child. One thing is for certain, though, you will be judged by other parents. They may talk about you, try to put you down, and they may stop inviting you to their children's birthday parties. You parent in your own style, according to your means and the needs of your child. When someone compliments you on doing a good job of being a parent, appreciate that, and allow it to motivate you to continue being a good parent.

Don't impose rules and regulations onto your teenager just because you have seen other parents doing the same thing. Take a close look at their kids first before deciding to follow in those parents' footsteps. Are their children happy? Do they share a positive relationship with their teenagers? Does your teenager really require this new change in their lives? Ask yourself these important questions before you implement any new changes to your parenting style. Sometimes, what might work for other parents and teenagers will not work for you, and that is because every child is different. People are going to judge you: there is no way to avoid this. However, you should stop paying any attention to what everyone else thinks, and focus more on what is best for your child. The only approval you need on your parenting should come from your own teenager, not from other parents who don't have any clue as to what you are dealing with everyday.

Being Too Controlling

Parents often make the mistake of trying to control every aspect of their children's lives. From choosing the type of clothing their kids wear to telling their kids what to do and when to do it. It can be an exhausting task which involves a lot of planning and time to make sure that everything is going as desired. When your child is little, a lot of control is needed to make sure that they are well taken care of. However, once they become teenagers, a lot of that control eases away so that your child can learn about becoming independent. If you continue to control every aspect of their lives, how will they ever learn to do things for themselves? How will they learn about making their own decisions? How will they make mistakes so that they can learn from them? Once your child starts their journey through adolescence, they will begin to display signs that they no longer need your help with certain things.

Parents must keep an eye out for these signs, because it indicates that your teenager wants to start taking control of their own lives. Sometimes, your teenager might make decisions that you are not happy with. For example, your teenage son might not want to study for his upcoming science test, and despite you asking him to make some time to learn, he brushes you off. If he chooses not to study, that is his own decision, and he must face the consequences. All you can do as a parent is motivate him to try, but ultimately it's his choice if he wants to study or not. Your child isn't your puppet, and you cannot pull the strings and expect them to do anything you want. Eventually, your child is going to grow up and develop a mind of their own. When this happens, you have to take a few steps back and allow them to explore life and make mistakes. There are teenagers who develop issues with anger and frustration because they feel trapped under their parents' control.

Being a Friend Rather Than a Parent

Every parent wants to be their child's closest friend. You want to gain their trust and be there for them whenever they need you. However, there are some parents who take it too far. They don't know when to draw the line, and when this happens, teenagers start taking advantage of their parents. We understand that you want to be a part of your teenager's life and you are afraid that they might forget about you when they make new friends and start doing new things. But a parent must understand that there are roles to be fulfilled, and that they cannot put aside their parental duties and take on the personality of a teenager. Yes, you can have fun moments with your teenager. Go out shopping together, do some bowling, go dancing, and watch funny movies. These are some pretty cool things that you can do with your teenager without having to bend the rules or go out of your role as a parent.

When you don't draw a line between friendship and parenting, your teenager may become too comfortable with the idea of you not setting rules and following through with them. Your teenager needs a parent, not another best friend. You don't have to worry about whether your teenager likes you or not, as long as they have someone who is looking out for them with their best interests at heart. There is a time for being friendly with your teenager, and there is time to be serious. As a parent, your role is to raise your child according to certain standards and rules that will teach them about life and prepare them for what is to come. Drinking alcohol and doing drugs with your teenager is not acceptable at all. There are some parents who engage in this type of behavior because they are so desperate to gain the approval of their teenagers, especially when they have had their kids at a young age. They want to have fun and live out their teenage years with their kids, without understanding how it can impact the relationship between parent and child.

Teenagers and COVID-19

COVID-19 has had a major impact on the lives of people around the world. We had to adjust to so much change within a short period of time, and we can no longer do things the way we used to do them before. This pandemic has taken a toll on our social lives, especially for teenagers who thrive among the presence of their friends. So many important aspects of their lives have been disrupted because of this virus. From their schooling life, to their social life; even their health has been affected. Let's explore how COVID-19 has altered the lives of teenagers, causing them to miss out on a lot of their lives.

How Did COVID Impact the Education System?

Schools around the world were impacted by the COVID-19 pandemic. In 2020, schools were forced to close immediately to help prevent the rapid spread of this deadly virus. Kids had to stop attending classes and stay home until further notice was given. Everything came to a standstill, and they were unable to cooperate with their teachers to continue any learning from home. All people could focus on was the rising death toll for those who had contracted the virus, and soon it became a battle of survival for each one of us. School was completely forgotten about because it was not a part of the basic essentials needed for survival. By the time it was considered safe for kids to go back to school, there had been so much time lost that teachers didn't know where to start. Before any of the kids could go back to school again, online classes became an option for a lot of people out there who had access to the internet. Schools were developing a system by which teachers could still educate their learners via an online portal. This would help bring learners up to speed with their syllabus so that they would not waste another year.

The problem was that by the time these schools had their systems up and running, a lot of teenagers had completely lost their focus and willingness to learn. It became difficult to adjust to studying from home, especially when there were so many distractions around. Being stuck at home with their family members became difficult for many teenagers to adapt to. They had no privacy to study, there was always noise all around, and they just could not concentrate. Online learning does not provide the same one-on-one assistance as classroom-based learning does. Teenagers need to be monitored and encouraged daily to finish their lessons and get their assignments completed. Without the supervision of a teacher, teenagers became more lazy, and they didn't take their work seriously.

The routine that they once followed allowed them to set aside time to study. Their entire day revolved around going to school, and this sudden change, brought on by the Coronavirus, had completely changed their routine. Their brains became lazy, and this affected the way they responded to their work once they were able to return to school. Once school was re-opened, high school learners were placed under a tremendous amount of pressure. They were bombarded with assignments and tests that were necessary for them to complete on time because they had to be promoted to the next grade. So much work, so little time. Can you imagine how stressful this must have been for these teenagers? This stress also contributed to the anger and rebellion that you see in your teenager. They are still young, and they are still learning how to deal with stress and how to adjust to fast-changing situations. Sometimes it can become very frustrating to do all of this in a short amount of time.

How did COVID-19 Impact a Teenager's Social Life?

A teenager depends heavily on their friends. They spend the majority of their time hanging out with friends and doing things that teenagers typically do. While spending so much time together, teenagers grow very close to their friends. They share secrets, have fun together, help each other, and grow together every day. When the pandemic hit, people were told to cut off all contact with those who were not a part of their immediate family. Complete isolation, no physical contact with the outside world, which meant no more hanging out with friends. Such an instant separation caused many teenagers to become depressed and lonely during the lockdown period. Yes, they could still text their friends and video call, but it just wasn't the same as physically getting out of the house and spending time together. Teenage years are for exploring and having fun, and being stuck at home all day did more harm than good for a teenager's self-confidence. As much as they wanted to stay safe from the virus, they also wanted to reconnect with their peers. The excitement of going out and doing fun stuff with their friends had disappeared, and all they can do now is sit at home and watch TV. Teenagers depend heavily on these social moments with their friends because it gives them the freedom to be who they are, away from home.

Teenagers have confessed that the lack of interaction with their friends has caused them to lose interest in certain activities and hobbies that they previously loved doing. The only kind of social life that still existed was that on social media. This was the only way teenagers could connect with one another, and it often required having access to a phone and a sufficient data connection. This must have been costly to parents who were out of jobs and not earning a salary during the lockdown. There might have been days when their parents could not afford to pay for their cell phone expenses, and as a result they had to lose touch with their friends. The fear of being forgotten to becoming socially excluded sets in, causing teenagers to become anxious and depressed. Let's be honest, friends make life a lot more exciting. Even as adults, we enjoy spending time with our peers because they make us happy and help us enjoy life. The same applies to teenagers; without their friends, life comes to a standstill.

The dating scene was also heavily impacted by the COVID-19 lockdown, and many teenagers could not go on dates. They weren't able to meet anyone new, either, because they were restricted from going out in public. If they were interested in someone, all they were able to do was chat on social media and see each other via video calls. This is a huge deal for teenagers, because dating is one of the major aspects of being a teenager. If a teenager identifies as LGBTQ, but has not yet come out to their parents, then being stuck in the house and unable to go out would have been extremely suffocating for them. The only chance they would have to be themselves and be free is when they leave the house and mingle with other LGBTQ teenagers. The social aspect of many teenagers' lives were completely ruined because of COVID-19, and most of these teenagers haven't fully recovered from it.

How COVID-19 Impacted a Teenager's Mental Health

COVID-19 has negatively impacted millions of people's lives worldwide, causing depression, anxiety, and other kinds of mental health conditions. Teenagers have also fallen prey to the venomous bite of COVID-19 and its consequences that we all are left to bear. During the lockdown, teenagers were forced to stay with their family members 24/7, without any break or chance to get away. There were many cases of suicide and domestic violence that were reported during the pandemic. Being stuck in the house with abusive parents or family members, or exposed to violence and substance abuse daily can cause a lot of anxiety and depression in teenagers. They cannot escape, they have nowhere to go to, and they can't even turn to their friends for support because they are forced to stay in the house. You cannot even begin to imagine how traumatizing that could be for a teenager. To witness abuse, or to be abused by someone in their family all the time, it can really mess up their sanity. This is why so many teenagers were pushed to commit suicide. They felt they had no other way out, and they could not stand another day of abuse. This is the kind of emotional pain that stays with you for a lifetime, and it can affect every aspect of your life for years to come.

Apart from being exposed to abuse on a daily basis, teenagers also develop mental health issues because of being isolated from their friends and family. Many teenagers lost people who were very important to them because of the COVID-19 virus. They were not allowed to attend the funeral to say goodbye as per COVID regulations. Imagine losing someone you love and not being able to say goodbye to them one last time.

Teenagers can easily feel trapped when they are stuck in a situation for long periods of time. When this happens, they can begin to develop panic attacks and anxiety disorders. Facing grief alone can be extremely depressing, especially for a teenager who is newly learning how to regulate their emotions. Being thrown into the deep end, suddenly, can push a teenager to their limits. Unfortunately, their mental health takes a bad hit, and it becomes difficult for these teenagers to reverse the damage that has been done already. If they don't receive professional help in time, the depression and anxiety can cause a lot of damage that will take a long time to heal. This can affect all areas of their lives, including their career, their personality, and their relationships.

Helping Your Teenager Cope During the Lockdown

It can be exhausting for parents to help their teenagers practice safety during this pandemic. Wearing masks, sanitizing hands, and social distancing are the basic safety and hygiene requirements that we all have to follow nowadays. However, it can be irritating for most teenagers. Most countries have imposed strict regulations with regard to the number of people that are allowed to enter certain places. There was even a curfew that had to be adhered to, and people could not be seen out in public after a certain time. As frustrating as this must have been for adults, it would have also been very frustrating for teenagers, because they spend most of their time outside of the home with friends. Teenagers and rules don't go very well together. All of these extra rules and regulations imposed on them, because of COVID, became suffocating to them. They aren't mature enough to understand the gravity of the situation. All they can see is that they are being held back from living life the way they want to. So when your teenager is so frustrated about it all, it will be hard to get them to adhere to certain safety measures that you, as a parent, have set in place in your home.

Apart from this, parents need to find ways to help their teenagers cope during lockdown. Even though the lockdown has now passed, there is no certainty that there won't be another one in the future. This pandemic is so unpredictable that no one can be sure about how normal our lives are going to be. The best thing parents should do is be prepared to help their teenager cope with another lockdown. You are an adult; you are mature and equipped to handle the stress and frustration that comes with being under lockdown, so you can help your teenager prepare themselves as well. Here are a few tips on how parents can help their teenager cope during a lockdown.

Firstly, Be Kind To Yourself

Your teenager will only cope as well as you do. If you want your teenager to stay calm throughout this stressful and scary time, then you will also have to try and remain calm. Parents don't realize that their children look to them for understanding during a confusing time. You cannot tell your child to stay calm when you are anxious and panicky all of the time. They will pick up on your facial expressions, body language, and on your overall demeanor, so don't even bother trying to play dual roles with them. Being strong and confident in front of your kids, but being scared and anxious behind their back, is only going to make things worse for you and your teenager. How long are you going to keep up the act?

Be kind to yourself. Make some time for yourself, so that you can work on processing your emotions. Find someone to talk to, someone who will help you through these tough emotions. Once you find a way to deal with your own fears and depression, then you can work on helping your teenager. If you don't have any family or friends to talk to, try to reach out to a helpline—there are plenty available. Your mental health is just as important as your teenager's. You have to make your child feel secure, and the only way you can do this is if you show that you are in control. When your teenager sees you scared and depressed, they begin to feel insecure and vulnerable, which leads to all sorts of anger and emotional issues in them.

Connect With Your Teenager

It is fundamental that parents and guardians establish a good connection with their children. However, it is during a crisis that parents and their children need to maintain their connection more than ever. Parents have to take notice of the way their teenager behaves during this time, and they should have regular conversations with their children about how they are coping with the stress of being under lockdown. You should understand that your teenager is missing out on a very important phase in their lives, and that they are away from their friends. They will need your support and comfort during this time, so don't ignore them or give them too much space to be on their own. Try to connect with your teenager by talking about the pandemic. Ask them how they feel about the lockdown, and about the Coronavirus. This will show them that you are thinking about their feelings.

Encourage your teenager to open up and talk freely about their feelings, and listen closely whenever they share their emotions with you. Try not to cut them off while they are speaking, and try not to correct them, either. Allow them to express themselves in their own way. The moment you try to correct them, or cut them off, they will instantly pull away from you. Be patient with your teenager. They might respond to your questions with a bit of attitude. However, try to maintain your composure and allow them to vent in their own way, just as long as they aren't being disrespectful. Take note of your teenager's feelings. Pay attention to the things that they say, and how they say it makes them feel when they talk about these things. If your teenager doesn't have much knowledge about the pandemic, you can help them understand the facts in a more loving way. Share with them your knowledge about the virus, and answer any of the questions that they might have.

Offer Hope and Support

The most important part of helping your child cope through this pandemic is by offering hope and support, even when your teenager refuses to accept it. Just telling them that you are there for them, whether they need you or not, provides them with security and makes them feel safe. Teenagers will feel scared and worried about their friends and family members. A killer virus has just been released onto the Earth, and people are dying within a matter of weeks. No one knows anything about this virus, and no one has a cure. That is a lot of information to process, especially for a teenager. At the end of the day, it's our job as parents to support our kids through this and make sure that they are dealing with their emotions in a healthy way.

Sometimes, parents become wrapped up in their own feelings, and they lose sight of their child's pain. It is hard for parents as well, because they have the responsibility of protecting their kids from this deadly virus. So, there will be times when they won't pay attention to the signs that indicate something more or different is going on with their teenager. When this happens, teenagers feel ignored, or unimportant. It adds to their feelings of depression, and they begin to feel alone. Eventually, thoughts of suicide crawl into their minds, and they have no one to talk to about these feelings. This can be avoided, only if parents go above and beyond to show their teenagers that they are there to support them whenever they need. The concern and love you shower onto your child will make a difference in the end. Don't ever think that your love means nothing to your teenager, because even though they might not show it, they do appreciate it on the inside.

Chapter 6:
Rebuilding Your Relationship With Your Teenager

Healing Wounds and Opening Hearts

I see you standing over there, staring down at the broken pieces of a relationship that you once shared with your teenager. You remember the days when they were little, running around the house with nothing but their underwear on. The warm cuddles on a winter's night, the cutest smiles they greeted you with every morning, and the heartbreaking moments when they were sick and wanted you by their side constantly. These were the most beautiful days as a parent, but somehow you feel as if the best days are behind you. You now have a teenager who avoids contact with you every chance they get. No more sitting down at a table and having supper together, now your teenager wants to eat in their room. No more late night conversations about sweet nothings, now your teenager ignores you whenever you try to talk to them.

I know it hurts, but it isn't going to be this way always. Your teenager needs some time to learn how to control their emotions. Their anger and frustration is a normal part of being a teenager. There is going to be happiness in your future, and you will salvage the special bond you shared with your teenager. They will always be your little boy or girl, no matter how grown up they become. But it's time to start treating them like the adults they so desperately want to become. Babying your teenager will only make things worse. Your wounds can heal, and you can move on from all of the damage that has been caused to your relationship. This can only happen if you both open up your hearts to each other and agree to work on your relationship. In this chapter, we focus on repairing the damage and rebuilding the relationship to make it even stronger this time around. Get ready, because there's some serious healing about to go down.

The Wrong Parenting Styles

Everyone is unique, and we all have our own way of doing things, That includes parenting as well. In this modern day, parents have started to embrace a whole new meaning of parenting that isn't based on rules and regulations. However, there are still parents out there who are using the wrong approach to parenting, and they don't even realize it. Now, we aren't here to judge anyone—none of us are perfect, and we all make mistakes. So if you notice that you have any of these styles in the way you parent, then you should really consider changing as soon as you can. Once you are aware of what might be contributing to the problem, it's time to take action and be a part of the solution. Below, we have listed a few popular parenting styles that are the root cause of a lot of issues between parent and child. Read through them and make notes about the things you find familiar in the way you parent. Remember, there is no judgment here, only support and care.

The Stubborn Parent

Yes, people can be stubborn at times. It's human nature. We all become a bit defiant and selfish from time to time. We like things to go our way, and we tend to like to have control over every aspect of our lives. It's either "my way or the highway," as most people would like to describe it. Even as parents, we want to maintain complete control over our kids. According to us, we are the only ones who know what's good for our children; and we remain steadfast in our beliefs, come what may. Have you ever stopped to think about where your beliefs came from? Were they passed down from your parents or grandparents? Or have you developed your own parenting style? Knowing what inspired the manner in which you parent your children is very important when trying to find a potential flaw in your parenting style. The era in which you were raised and when you were a child is very different from the day and age we are living in now.

Parents tend to forget this significant detail, and they often impose their olden-day parenting styles onto their modern-day teenagers. We are not saying that you were raised in the wrong way. Your parents knew exactly what to do to make sure that you grew up well, as the world was different back then. Today, a lot has changed. The world has evolved so much, and people's beliefs have changed as well. Your teenager is living in a very different time than you were when you were younger. The rules that worked on you will not necessarily work on your teenager. This is what so many parents cannot understand. They lose touch with reality, and become stuck in the olden days, which blindsides them from being the kind of parents their teenagers need today.

The Proud Parent

There is no dearth of prideful parents living among us these days. It's hard to miss them, especially when they go out of their way to make themselves known. Parents who are proud and vain often like to talk about themselves. They boast about what good parents they are, and how their kids always excel at everything they do. Don't get me wrong, all parents have the right to boast about this. But when it comes to these proud parents, they boast with the intention of putting other parents down. They want people to admire them and envy their lives, so they always try to be better than others. However, in reality, their kids are miserable and depressed. They don't have a relationship with their teenagers, and they don't really care about their kids' feelings, as long as everything works out in their favor.

Being proud of your child's accomplishments and giving yourself a little credit for it as well is a normal part of parenting. You do work hard and you deserve to be happy and proud of the way you raise your kids. As long as you are doing it in a way that motivates and uplifts other parents, and makes your children happy, this is fine. Parents who hold themselves in high regard, lose the respect of their teenagers, or worse, raise their children to become just like that? There is no positive side to parenting in that manner, because it is a selfish way to raise your children. These types of parents pressure their children to keep up perfect grades, perfect figures, and perfect hobbies. And they get them to do all of this all because they want to "look good" as parents. They don't think about what their children really want. All they think about is their image and reputation.

The Overprotective Parent

This is the most common type of parenting style there is. Almost 75% of parents admit to being paranoid and overprotective of their children (Cross, 2019). It's normal for parents to worry about their teenagers, and to think about what they are doing, who they are with, or whether they are safe. It's the motherly instinct to always feel like your child needs you and that they can't function without you on their own. However, this is far from the truth for teenagers. They want nothing more than to be left alone, which is impossible if you have an overprotective parent. As they get older, teenagers require their alone time so that they can figure out the world on their own. They don't want to be questioned constantly on their whereabouts, or on their dressing, or about who they're friends with.

When parents become overbearing, teenagers will shut them out to protect their own peace. They don't want to be told what to do all of the time, and they don't want to be monitored daily. They want to feel more independent and in control of their own lives, which is a good thing for their development. When you restrict your teenager from going out with their friends, or from wearing clothing that they chose to express themselves, it makes them feel upset and frustrated. They feel like you don't trust them to go out on their own, or to dress the way they want to. They don't realize that you are restricting them because you want to keep them safe. They see other parents allowing their teenagers to do things that are normal for teenagers, yet their own parents hold them back from being a part of this. Your teenager isn't a child anymore. They are growing up to become young adults, so try and treat them like one.

The Absent Parent

The term "absent parent" can take on many forms. It can describe a parent who works a lot and has no time for their children, or it can describe a parent who is hung up on substances all of the time and is unable to parent their kids. It can also be used to describe a parent who is there physically, but emotionally they are unavailable for their children. Whatever the situation might be, if a parent isn't there physically or emotionally for their kids, they are considered an absent parent. It doesn't matter if you are at home all day, cleaning, cooking, and making sure everything is spick and span. You are probably there to send your kids off to school, and you are there when they return in the afternoon. You lay out hot meals for them, and you draw them relaxing baths before bedtime. But, do you spend time having a conversation with them? Do you pray over them before bedtime? Can you tell which one of your kids is being bullied at school? Do you have a good relationship with your kids individually?

These are important questions you should ask yourself. Take some time to sit down and think about the relationship you share with your teenager. Are you an absent parent? Do you spend a lot of your time working? Are you ignoring your teenager unknowingly? Have you been separated from your spouse and hardly get time to see your kids? Parents don't realize how much their absence affects their children. They look to you for love and support, and when they don't get this from you, they begin to search for it elsewhere. That's when they become involved with sex, drugs, and alcohol. Parents push their kids away by not paying attention to them, and this drives them to search for love and attention in other places. Once they find what they are looking for in these other places, it becomes very hard to convince them to move away from them.

The Judgmental Parent

The last thing a teenager needs is a parent who judges everything they do. This is the time for teenagers to make mistakes and learn from them on their own, so it's obvious that they are not always going to make the right decisions. Some parents are always nagging their kids, telling them what to wear, how to behave, or comparing them to other teenagers and expecting them to behave in the same manner. They don't realize that they are coming across as being judgmental to their teenagers, and this is the reason why teenagers pull back from these types of parents. Saying things like, "You're being too emotional, it's time to grow up now," or, "I don't like the way you are walking," are some common things that parents say to their kids which come across as being judgmental. Sometimes, parents get too comfortable saying these things to their kids, and they don't understand that their child is becoming a young adult.

You cannot say certain things without thinking how it will affect your teenager. They aren't children anymore, so we as parents have to change the way we speak to them. Try not to sound judgmental when you are offering advice to your teen. Even though you mean well, they might perceive all of your questions and unsolicited advice as you passing judgment on them and telling them how to live their lives. At this age, they are very emotional and angry, so they really don't need you judging them or picking on every little thing that they do. The more picky and judgy you are, the further away your teenager will go from you. You will lose the connection you have, all because you didn't know what to say or how to say it. Parents must learn when to keep their opinions to themselves, especially when their teenager is experiencing issues with their self-esteem. If you don't have anything good to say, or any advice to help them find a solution, then it's best to just remain quiet.

How to Repair a Broken Relationship With Your Teenager

Do you have a broken relationship with your teenager? Is there a distance that has been increasing between you? Are you not sure who your child is anymore? Well, you're not the only parent who's going through this. Literally every parent of a teenager knows exactly what it's like to miss the relationship they once had with their children. Now that they are in their teenage years, it's hard to relate to them. Over time, your relationship gets colder and more distant, until one day you realize that you don't know who your child is anymore. Their favorite color has changed, they don't like eating Fruit Loops for breakfast anymore, and they prefer to spend time alone rather than with you. These changes can be shocking to parents, and sometimes it can even hurt them because they feel as if they lost their child along the way.

No matter how bad the relationship might be, it can be fixed. There is a way for you to repair the bond you once shared with your teenager. However, for that to happen, you must be willing to change your attitude towards your teenager. You have to see things through a new pair of eyes, without passing judgment on your teenager. We will help you get back to your roots as a parent. Reconnect with your teenager and try to see things from their point of view so that you can understand them better. Before you proceed to read the advice below, make sure that you are in a good place emotionally and mentally. This journey won't be easy, but you can achieve success if you just stay committed.

Step 1: Analyze the Current State of Your Relationship With Your Teen

It's important to gain a good understanding of where you are right now in your role as a parent. Do you feel confident in yourself? How is your relationship with your teenager? Take stock of the good and the bad that now exists between you two. Analyze the dynamic of your relationship, and write down all of the things that you agree on. Also make note of issues that cause your opinions to clash. These are usually the things that lead to major misunderstandings and arguments. Once you have a clear picture of how bad the damage is, you can now take the necessary steps to undo that damage. You cannot skip this step thinking that you already have a good idea of what the issues are and how bad they've become. You have to sit down and evaluate every aspect of your relationship and question every incident that has ever occurred.

Your teenager might remember something that you completely forgot. It could be something you said, or an event that had a huge impact on their lives. It would be a good idea to sit down and speak to your teenager about their feelings. Try to find out what their issues are, and don't downplay their pain or experiences in any way. If you truly want to heal your relationship, you must be willing to listen and take in all of the information that your teenager is giving you. I know this isn't easy. It's probably the most difficult step in your journey. However, it is the most important, and you should be 100% open to finding out the truth. You can take down notes in a journal, or you can create a survey for your teenager and you to fill out. This method might work best to help you be truthful about your experiences. Sometimes, it can be hard to open up face to face, so putting your emotions down on paper may be more welcomed.

Step 2: Own Up to Your Mistakes

Another significant step in the whole process is accepting fault and taking responsibility for your part in the whole problem. When you sit down and have a conversation with your teenager, they will reveal certain issues to you where you play the villain of their story. The last thing you want to do is become defensive, because this can take away any chance of you repairing the relationship between you and your teenager. I know that it can be heartbreaking to see that you were the one who caused the problems that have now blown out of proportion. It's a tough pill to swallow, accepting all of that blame, but you have to do it if you want to start the healing process. Parents who have a hard time accepting their part in the problem might be experiencing issues with maturity. There are a lot of parents out there who aren't mature, even though they are raising teenagers.

Somehow, these parents are still stuck in their own childish ways, and they continue to shift blame or deny it altogether. When you deflect blame, you miss the opportunity to learn from your mistakes. Unless you accept your faults, you can never truly grow as a human being, and you will be stuck in that toxic circle for the rest of your life. One of the major reasons why parents don't accept blame is because they have too much pride to admit that they were wrong. There is a notion that parents are always right, and that they always know what is best for their children. While this may be true to a certain extent, there are situations where parents mess up along the way. If you are afraid that your teenager would take advantage of the fact that you made a mistake, then you really need to step up your game as a parent. You can accept blame without making yourself vulnerable to being used by your teenager. The only way you can do this is if you are confident in yourself.

Step 3: Develop a Plan of Action

The next step in your healing journey would be to develop a plan of action. Now that you are aware of what the problems are between you and your teenager, you can focus on coming up with a solution to each of these problems. Sometimes, it might be hard for you to even hold a conversation with your teenager, let alone find solutions to the issues. So it may be a good idea if you both decided to undergo family counseling with a professional who will be able to help you find the cracks in your relationship. Our anger and resentment can get the best of us at times, and this causes us to become blind and to overlook the concerns that are staring us in our face. A trained counselor or therapist can help you see past the anger. They have their methods of helping people, and because they are not emotionally involved, they can see the bigger picture without being biased. You can even work with your therapist to come up with solutions to these problems. The plan of action has to be developed according to each person's ability to see it through. Start off with baby steps to see how your teenager reacts to it, because it can be too much to deal with if you start off by expecting them to do more than they can handle.

Everything takes time, which is important for the healing process as well. You should develop all plans with good timing. Don't rush and expect things to change overnight; always remember that change takes time, and you should be able to apply that to your timeline as well. When things are done according to good timing, you have a greater chance at succeeding in your plans. Don't skip the baby steps and immediately jump to the last step, thinking that you will find the same success. You most definitely would have to start all over again from scratch, so be patient with your teenager and with yourself. Take your teenager's needs and feelings into consideration while developing a plan of action. You have a better chance of succeeding if your teenager is open and receptive towards the plan. Rebellion will only delay the healing process, and can end up making things worse.

Step 4: Review and Evaluate Your Performance

Last, but not least, make sure that you evaluate your plan consistently throughout the process. You can work with your therapist and figure out a way to assess and track your progress from home. Your therapist might suggest using a journal to write down your experiences daily, and at the end of the week you can read through each day and see whether you have been getting better or worse. Write down whatever obstacles you faced along the way; it can help to point out where the issues lie. As you identify new issues, develop plans to tackle them as well during the process. Take your teenager out for lunch at the end of the week, and speak to them about their progress as well. It's good to understand how well the plan has been working for them also, so that you can tweak the plan wherever necessary to make sure that you both are comfortable and growing at your own pace.

Practical Exercises to Help You Become a Better Parent

Developing a plan of action can be a bit confusing to some parents. You wouldn't know where to begin and where to end. Fear not, for we have developed some great exercises to help you become a better parent to your teenager. You can incorporate these exercises into your daily lives. Take what you need and feel free to add more if you'd like. Below, you will find a few great practical exercises to help you improve on your parenting skills. Are you ready for change? Let's go!

Judge Less, Compliment More

I don't think parents realize how many times a day they complain or judge the things that their kids do. However, I know for a fact that their kids will be able to tell you the exact number of times their parents pinpoint their flaws in a day. You see, teenagers pay close attention to how their parents react to the things they do. They are innocently looking to see just how much their parents love them and notice the things they do. Your teenager walks into the house with a test sheet that shows how much they improved since the last semester. However, instead of recognizing their improvement, you start questioning them about why they haven't achieved an A on their test. This is a common example of what parents do to put their kids down and demotivate them from becoming better. Next time, consider complimenting your teenager and saying, "Well done on getting better results. I know you will do even better in the future." That's all it takes. You don't have to go out of your way to be judgmental; there are ways that you can get your message across in a loving manner, too.

Make Time for Your Teenager

Just because your teenager is growing into a young adult doesn't mean that you should stop spending time with them. They may become more distant and will want to spend a lot of time alone, but it's only because they are trying to figure out how to deal with all the changes happening to them. Don't misread this as them not wanting to spend time with you because they are all grown up now. Your teenager will always be your baby, no matter how big they get. Plan fun activities to do with them during the weekends or on school holidays. Show them that you can still have fun, even though they aren't little kids anymore. Play video games together, stay up late watching movies, talk about boys, and tell them about your high school experiences. Whatever it is that you decide to do is great, as long as you are spending genuine time with your teenager. Plan out your week, and be sure to include time for your child in your schedule.

Set Clear Boundaries and Explain Them to Your Teenager

Teenagers must understand that there are certain rules that have to be followed as long as they are living under your roof. Don't just set the rules suddenly and expect them to follow through with them. This would seem cold, and it won't look like it came from a place of love. This can make it harder for them to accept these rules. Sit down and explain to your teenager why you have set certain rules and boundaries. Help them see that you are not trying to control their lives, but that you are simply trying to make sure they are safe and that they develop good morals as human beings. When you help your teenager to see things from a different perspective, it enables them to open up and become more receptive to the rules you set.

Control Your Emotions and Be a Good Role Model

Children always walk in the footsteps of their parents. Even as teenagers, they watch the things that you do, and they follow suit. If you want your teenager to behave in a certain way and follow certain rules, you will have to be a role model for them first. The best way you can teach your child about life is by showing them how you live yours. Having control over your emotions is one of the big aspects of life, and how you react to situations is how your teenager will react to them as well. They look to you for guidance, and everything you do is important because they are watching your every move. If you don't want your teenager to become involved with violence, show them how to react to a situation that makes them angry. Set an example for them to follow; you cannot say one thing and then do something else.

Conclusion

You should now have a better understanding of why your teenager is always angry, especially after reading about all of the causes of teenage anger above. Now, I understand that it's not easy to mend a broken relationship, and that it can be a very emotional journey. But I have faith in you as a parent. I know that you want only the best for your child, and you are willing to do anything to make sure that your teenager is happy. It's going to be a long, winding road, but as long as you are committed to the process, there is no reason you should fail. Forget about the past, and embrace a new future with your teenager. Shift your focus onto fixing the relationship, and you will notice how fast things start to change for the better. Once you have your mind set on growth and change, nothing can stop you or hold you back from achieving success.

Your relationship with your teenager will get better. All you have to do is be more understanding towards your teenager, and be more confident in yourself as a parent. This phase will pass, and they will become young adults with a world of opportunity at their doorstep. Don't lose this time with them; instead, make the best of each day that you get to spend with your teenager. Teach them, encourage them, support them, but most of all, love them.

References

10 Tips to Help Easily Distractible Teens Focus. (2016, November 29). Weird, Unsocialized Homeschoolers. https://www.weirdunsocializedhomeschoolers.com/distractible-teens/

10 Ways to a Better Relationship with Your Teenager | Families for Life. (n.d.). Familiesforlife.sg. https://familiesforlife.sg/discover-an-article/Pages/10-Ways-to-a-Better-Relationship-with-Your-Teenager.aspx

Cross, J. (2019, August 8). *What Does Too Much Screen Time Do to Kids' Brains?* NewYork-Presbyterian. https://healthmatters.nyp.org/what-does-too-much-screen-time-do-to-childrens-brains/

Forster, K. (2017, February 22). *Secrets of the teenage brain.* The Guardian; The Guardian. https://www.theguardian.com/lifeandstyle/2015/jan/25/secrets-of-the-teenage-brain

Improve Your Parenting Skills These 7 Tips. (n.d.). Verywell Family. https://www.verywellfamily.com/improve-your-parenting-skills-3545045

Life as a Teenager. (n.d.). Retrieved February 6, 2022, from https://www.allpsychologycareers.com/teenagers/life-as-a-teenager/#:~:text=The%20life%20of%20a%20teenager%20seems%20to%20change%20daily.&text=Constantly%20exposed%20to%20new%20ideas

National Center for Victims of Crime. (n.d.). *Child Sexual Abuse Statistics – The National Center for Victims of Crime.* National Center for Victims of Crime. https://victimsofcrime.org/child-sexual-abuse-statistics/

Pahr, K. (2019, May 21). *Teenage Rebellion Isn't What it Used to Be — Here's How to Deal.* Parents; Parents. https://www.parents.com/parents-magazine/teenage-rebellion-causes-consequences-and-how-parents-can-deal/

Practice Parenting Skills | Essentials | Parenting Information | CDC. (2020, June 8). Www.cdc.gov. https://www.cdc.gov/parents/essentials/activities/index.html

Teens and Anger. (n.d.). Child Mind Institute. https://childmind.org/article/teens-and-anger/

The Kit_13/54. (2021, March 31). Pixabay. https://pixabay.com/photos/skateboard-skater-teen-style-6518594/

World Health Organization. (2021, November 17). *Adolescent mental health*. World Health Organization; World Health Organization: WHO. https://www.who.int/news-room/fact-sheets/detail/adolescent-mental-health

Image References

Collins, B. (2020, October 2). *Man in gray jacket sitting near window*. Unsplash.com. https://unsplash.com/photos/6UjejTrAVAw

Constance, K. (2017, September 1). *woman sitting on dock near water*. Unsplash.com. https://unsplash.com/photos/B4axGpyGHJk

CottonBro. (2020, March 27). *Teenage boy in hoodie*. Pexels.com. https://www.pexels.com/photo/boy-in-black-hoodie-standing-near-white-wall-4100481/

Cottonbro. (2020, June 25). Pexels.com. https://www.pexels.com/photo/woman-in-gray-shirt-smiling-4842486/

Dominigos, J. (2020, March 30). *woman in brown tank top*. Unsplash.com. https://unsplash.com/photos/QrU1apBxO5M

Engeland, S. (2016, October 26). *Woman sitting on bed with MacBook Air*. Unsplash.com. https://unsplash.com/photos/GwVmBgpP-PQ

Fewings, N. (2020, June 24). *Black and gray I love you print textile photo*. Unsplash.com. https://unsplash.com/photos/4pZu15OeTXA

Gabrowska, K. (2021, February 21). *Mother throws daughters phone.* Pexels.com. https://www.pexels.com/photo/mother-throws-daughter-s-phone-6957241/

Lach, R. (2021, May 29). *Mother smiling at her children.* Pexels.com. https://www.pexels.com/photo/mother-smiling-to-her-children-holding-digital-pad-9786310/

Nekrashevich, A. (2020, December 22). *Woman squeezing pimples with her fingers.* Pexels.com. https://www.pexels.com/photo/woman-squeezing-her-pimples-with-her-fingers-6476081/

Pham, D. (2018, June 16). *people holding shoulders sitting on the wall.* Unsplash.com. https://unsplash.com/photos/Cecb0_8Hx-o

Placabae, T. (2021, September 22). *Teenage girl with long black hair sitting on the floor.* Pexels.com. https://www.pexels.com/photo/teenage-girl-with-long-black-hair-sitting-on-floor-and-looking-sadly-at-camera-10910499/

Preez, P. D. (2020, November 9). *Person in black long sleeve shirt holding hands.* Unsplash.com. https://unsplash.com/photos/aPa843frIzI

Production, M. (2021, March 23). *Girl and boy standing on the stairs.* Pexels.com. https://www.pexels.com/photo/stairs-girl-man-drugs-7230356/

Ragfelt, O. (2018, January 20). *Boy sitting down.* Unsplash.com. https://unsplash.com/photos/k2T6qI1ZK1k

Reiner, Z. (2018, April 15). *Tree roots on rock formation.* Unsplash.com. https://unsplash.com/photos/hW11fwjzVfA

Uhas, G. (2021, October 11). *HD photo by Gaspar Uhas.* Unsplash.com. https://unsplash.com/photos/HdM5nQfCgEE

Wong, W. (2017, May 18). *Man standing in subway.* Unsplash.com. https://unsplash.com/photos/u7dy-n4uZVk